# Religious Fundamentalism and American Education

SUNY Series in
# PHILOSOPHY OF EDUCATION
*Philip L. Smith, Editor*

and

SUNY Series
# FRONTIERS IN EDUCATION
*Philip G. Altbach, Editor,*
*in cooperation with the Graduate School of Education,*
*State University of New York at Buffalo.*

The Frontiers in Education Series feaures and draws
upon a range of disciplines and approaches in the
analysis of educational issues and concerns, helping to
reinterpret established fields of scholarship in education
by encouraging the latest synthesis and research.

Other books in this series include:

*Class, Race, and Gender in American Education*
—Lois Weis (ed.)

*Excellence and Equality: A Qualitatively Different*
*Perspective on Gifted and Talented Education*
—David M. Fetterman

*Change and Effectiveness in Schools: A Cultural Perspective*
—Gretchen B. Rossman, H. Dickson Corbett,
and William A. Firestone

*The Curriculum: Problems, Politics, and Possibilities*
—Landon E. Beyer and Michael W. Apple (eds.)

*Religious Fundamentalism*
*and*
*American Education*

The Battle for the Public Schools

Eugene F. Provenzo, Jr.

*State University of New York Press*

Published by
State University of New York Press, Albany

© 1990   State University of New York

For information, address State University of New York
Press, State University Plaza, Albany, N.Y., 12246

Library of Congress Cataloging-in-Publication Data

Provenzo, Eugene F.
    Religious fundamentalism and American education : the battle for
the public schools / Eugene F. Provenzo, Jr.
        p.   cm. — (SUNY series in philosophy of education) (SUNY
series, frontiers in education)
        Bibliography: p.
        ISBN 0-7914-0217-7. — ISBN 0-7914-0218-5 (pbk.)
        1. Church and education—United States. 2. Public schools—United
States. 3. Fundamentalism. I. Title. II. Series. III. Series:
SUNY series, frontiers in education.
LC111.P83   1990
371'.01'0973—dc20                                                      89-4456
                                                                       CIP


10 9 8 7 6 5 4 3 2

*For*
*Gary N. McCloskey, O.S.A.,*
*student, friend, and colleague*

# Contents

# Introduction

During the past decade a powerful religious and social movement that has its origins in the Christian evangelical tradition has reemerged in the United States. It describes itself as being "anti-evolution," "pro-life," "pro-family" and "pro-school prayer." It is opposed to the doctrine of the Separation of Church and State and what it believes to be a growing secularization of American society. The movement is well-funded and closely aligned with the New Political Right.

The attitudes and opinions of this movement have been most clearly formulated and articulated by those individuals loosely known within the Christian evangelical tradition as fundamentalists, or perhaps more accurately ultra-fundamentalists.[1] This book is about the ultra-fundamentalist movement and its impact on American education.

The ultra-fundamentalists represent an important force in contemporary American education and culture. One need only pick up a recent magazine or newspaper—or turn on a television—to realize the extent to which this is true. Jerry Falwell, the former leader of the Moral Majority, was featured on the cover of *Time* magazine, was invited to the White House, and appeared regularly on national television. Television ministries under the direction of ultra-fundamentalist ministers such as Pat Robertson are broadcast throughout the country. The sexual indiscretions of Jim Bakker, the former head of the "Praise the Lord" (P.T.L.) ministry and another television minister, Jimmy Swaggart, gain national attention. Mel and Norma Gabler, self-appointed textbook censors, are the subject of numerous articles in educational journals and the popular press.

In Congress, ultra-fundamentalist groups have lobbied for the passage of legislation supporting school prayer and tuition-tax credits for private schools. They received the support of President Reagan in their attempt to introduce Creationism as a part of the regular biology curriculum of the public schools. On a local level, ultra-fundamentalist groups have pressured public schools to censure textbooks, to ban homosexuals from teaching, to eliminate sex education from the curriculum and to remove what they consider to be objectionable reading materials from public school libraries.

As this work will attempt to demonstrate, the ultra-fundamentalists have a clearly articulated vision of culture and education. While the author disagrees with many of their conclusions, he feels that they have raised important questions concerning the role that the public schools play in promoting specific political and social ideologies; the rights of parents to determine what their children will learn; and whether or not the schools should teach values. What unites the various ultra-fundamentalist groups—despite their doctrinal differences and internal politics—is a clear and consistent belief that American culture, and ultimately Christianity, is being subverted by what they describe as the philosophy of "secular humanism."

## THE ULTRA-FUNDAMENTALISTS' WAR
## AGAINST SECULAR HUMANISM

Following the landslide political victory of Ronald Reagan in the 1980 presidential election, the Moral Majority and other ultra-fundamentalist groups increasingly focused their attention on what they described as the threat of secular humanism. According to Tim LaHaye, a board member of the Moral Majority and one of the most influential ultra-fundamentalist spokesmen, secular humanism represents:

> man's attempt to solve his problems independently of God. Since moral conditions have become worse in direct proportion to humanism's influence, which has moved our country from a biblically based society to an amoral, "democratic society" during the past forty years, one would think that the humanists would realize the futility of their position. To the contrary, they treacherously refuse to face the reality of their failures, blaming them instead on traditional religion or ignorance or capitalism or religious superstitions.[2]

Secular humanism is perceived by ultra-fundamentalists such as LaHaye, as being consciously anti-Christian. It is seen as supporting everything from evolutionary theory to pornography, from sexual promiscuity to socialism. Media, education and government are seen by the ultra-fundamentalists as being dominated by supporters of secular humanism. Jerry Falwell has described secular humanism as having become the new religion of America, taking the place of the Bible.[3] Francis A. Schaeffer, perhaps the most articulate and literate of the ultra-fundamentalist leaders, has argued that the:

> Humanists have been determined to beat to death the knowledge of God and the knowledge that God has not been silent, but has spoken in the Bible and through Christ—and they have been determined to do this even though the death of values has come with the death of that knowledge.[4]

Clearly people such as Schaeffer feel that the values that they believe are the most important are threatened by the supposedly anti-Christian nature of humanist thought and inquiry.

Important political leaders have lent their support to the antihumanist movement of the ultra-fundamentalists. Senator Jesse Helms, for example, in his introduction to Homer Duncan's book *Secular Humanism: the Most Dangerous Religion in America* explains that:

> When the U.S. Supreme Court prohibited children from participating in voluntary prayers in public schools, the conclusion is inescapable that the Supreme Court not only violated the right of free exercise of religion for all Americans; it also established a national religion in the United States—the religion of secular humanism.[5]

Religious leaders such as Tim LaHaye maintain that the foundations of the American political system are essentially Christian and that government must be recaptured from the debilitating influence of humanist thought.[6] Ignoring the influence of pre-Christian philosophers such as Polybius and Aristotle, who outlined in their works, republican theories of government based upon a system of checks and balances, LaHaye maintains that:

> Our unique check-and-balance system of government would never have been conceived by humanism. It is borrowed directly from Scripture.[7]

The Puritan work ethic, free enterprise, the private ownership of land and capitalism have, according to LaHaye, evolved exclusively from Biblical teaching.[8]

In *The Battle for the Mind* LaHaye maintains that there are 272,000 humanists in the United States who have taken control of the national media, newspapers, magazines, government and education.[9] According to him, they have created a conspiracy to control the minds and hearts of the American people. Yet LaHaye and other ultra-fundamentalists fail to adequately identify the current leaders of the humanist movement in America. Most frequently they cite the work of the American Humanist

Association, and more specifically their publication of the *Humanist Manifesto I* (1933) and the *Humanist Manifesto II* (1973).[10]

The American Humanist Association can in no way be seen as being the primary representative of the humanist movement in America. Its 1973 *Humanist Manifesto II*, which was signed by Sidney Hook, B.F. Skinner, Isaac Asimov and others, denounced religion in favor of the "scientific method." In doing so, the *Humanist Manifesto II* and its signers set themselves apart from the mainstream of the Western humanist tradition which had, since the late Middle Ages and early Renaissance, been concerned with the question of man's ability to direct his own destiny and with his relationship with God.

Using the *Humanist Manifesto I and II* as his source, Homer Duncan argues that "Communism is humanism in political disguise."[11] According to Duncan, communism and secular humanism both deny supernatural and Divine revelation; both seek to control the educational system and both destroy all religions except their own; and finally, both seek the betterment of the human race and the promotion of world government.[12]

The ultra-fundamentalists maintain that secular humanism is a religion, and as such its influence should not be allowed in the public schools. For Duncan, humanism "deifies man and dethrones God."[13] Its purpose is to replace theism with humanism. At a much more sophisticated level, the theologian and historian Rousas J. Rushdoony argues that humanism is no less a religion than Christianity. Citing the philosopher Paul Tillich, he maintains that religion can be defined as an "ultimate concern" and thus includes both theistic and nontheistic approaches. In this case a theistic religion would be predicated on God as the central agent in the organization of the system, whereas in a nontheistic system God's place would be taken by the state or by man in general. According to Rushdoony, the denial of God does not eliminate the fact that there is an "operative god" in every religious system or faith. In the end he concludes that in the case of the United States:

> The religious motivation, impetus and fervor behind our present law structure, our state establishment of religion, is humanism.[14]

Arguments that attempt to substantiate the existence of a religion of secular humanism serve the function of creating a philosophical and social movement the ultra-fundamentalists can attack. By establishing secular humanism as the dominant philosophy underlying contemporary culture and education, and then by arguing that it is also a religion, the ultra-fundamentalists are able to discredit any arguments in favor of the Separation of Church and State. The logic is that if secular humanism is a religion it has no place as a philosophy influencing either our government or the curriculum of the public schools.

The contention that secular humanism exists as an identifiable philosophical movement, and furthermore as a religion, clearly has credence among many ultra-fundamentalist leaders. Francis A. Schaeffer in his work *A Christian Manifesto*, cites evidence from various Supreme Court cases of the 1960s to substantiate his view that secular humanism is a religion.[15] He refers, for example, to the 1965 Supreme Court case of the *United States v. Seger* in which it is argued by the court that the test of religious belief is a:

> sincere and meaningful belief which occupies in the life of its possessor a place parallel to that filled by the God of those admittedly qualifying for the exemption.[16]

Schaeffer (as do nearly all of the ultra-fundamentalist leaders), objects that so many tax supported activities contradict conservative Christian beliefs. Carl Sagan's public television series *Cosmos*, for example, maintained that: "The cosmos is all that ever is or ever will be."[17] Schaeffer argues that such an opinion clearly implies a denial of God and a specifically humanist or secular humanist outlook. In the same light, Schaeffer objects to documentaries on controversial issues such as abortion being funded by tax-supported groups including Public Television.[18]

The idea that secular humanism is a religion, or even a coherent philosophy, has little credence. According to standard dictionary definition, in this case *The American Heritage Dictionary of the English Language*, a religion (under the first definition) is: "The expression of man's belief in and reverence for a superhuman power recognized as the creator and governor of the universe."[19] Secular humanism, even as defined by the ultra-fundamentalists, does not place a "superhuman power" at its center.

In addition, unlike a movement such as Chinese Taoism, it cannot be identified with a coherent body of knowledge or set of intellectual or philosophical leaders: Who are the organizational leaders of the secular humanist movement? What are their major texts? Who are its current intellectual leaders? How is their work linked and connected?

To argue that the American Humanist Association somehow represents the leadership of a secular humanist movement, and to argue as the ultra-fundamentalists do that secular humanism is the major intellectual force shaping contemporary culture, is patently absurd. In the case of John Dewey (who is viewed by the ultra-fundamentalists as a leader of the movement), it is impossible to place his work in the limited context of what is defined as secular humanism, or to declare it to be part of a coherent religious system. Dewey's signing of a document such as the *Humanist Manifesto, I* does not imply that he shared a religious and philosophical viewpoint with its other signatories. John Dewey and Sidney Hook, for example, had widely different philosophical and ideological points of view. Yet both signed the *Humanist Manifesto, I.*

If anything can be defined as secular humanism, it is probably those values that exist outside of the context of ultra-fundamentalist absolute truths. Secular humanism is neither a coherent religion, nor philosophy. This does not mean, however, that the ultra-fundamentalists are not responding to what they perceive as powerful forces within the society that are, from their perspective, antireligious and ultimately "un-Christian." Secular humanism is for them a reality that manifests itself in the social problems and conflicts that are so much a part of contemporary American life. Contrary to many of the criticisms of the ultra-fundamentalists and their war against secular humanism, they are in fact responding to real problems and conflicts within our society. Many of the issues they have focused on are of concern to a much larger portion of the population than just the conservative Protestant religious tradition they represent. Nowhere is this clearer than in the case of the public schools.

## THE ULTRA-FUNDAMENTALIST CRITIQUE
## OF THE PUBLIC SCHOOLS

As a result of their fear of the threat of secular humanism, ultra-fundamentalists have set up their own private schools and lobbied for special tax privileges and exemptions for parents who send their children to their schools. At the same time, they have also tried to significantly influence what is taught in the public schools throughout the country. In general, the ultra-fundamentalists believe that "secular humanist" teachers, textbooks and curricula are instilling Godless values into America's children. Tim LaHaye, for example, argues that:

> Today, public education is so humanistic that it is both anti-Catholic and anti-Protestant—because it's anti-God. With the expulsion of God from the schools, the view that man was created by God and thus responsible for obeying His moral absolutes, deteriorated drastically....the chaos of today's public education system is in direct proportion to its religious obsession with humanism.[20]

Other ultra-fundamentalists hold similar views. Mel and Norma

Gabler, whose Texas based Educational Research Analysts organization is the major ultra-fundamentalist clearinghouse for the review of mainstream educational materials, maintain that the secular humanist movement in the public schools:

> not only defies Christian values and the authority of parents, but borders on treason and violates the U.S. Constitution by teaching a religion.[21]

Similar sentiments are expressed again and again by a wide-range of ultra-fundamentalist writers. Reverend Jerry Falwell in his book *America Can Be Saved* states that:

> One day, I hope in the next ten years, I can trust that we will have more Christian day schools than there are public schools. I hope I live to see the day when, as in the early days of our country, we won't have any public schools. The churches will have taken them over again and Christians will be running them. What a happy day that will be.[22]

Ultra-fundamentalist leaders feel strongly that the control of the content of education should be exclusively in the hands of parents and the family. The television evangelist Pat Robertson has argued that:

> The ultimate solution is that we have to get the state out of the business of educating kids at the primary and secondary levels, and get that education back in the hands of parents where it belongs.[23]

What concerns the ultra-fundamentalists is that the traditional social, political and religious value system to which they subscribe is no longer being supported in public institutions such as the schools. From their perspective, the issue of secular humanism in the public schools is by no means unreasonable or the creation a "straw man." As Julius Lester explains:

> It is too simple to maintain, as some do, that "secular humanism is a straw man. They are looking for someone to blame." Neither is it particularly illuminating to define the attacks on secular humanism as a new McCarthyism which is substituting humanists for "reds." It is not so simple because the underlying issue, first raised unintentionally by the *Brown* decision, is the all important one of collective identity, i.e., what does it mean to be American?[24]

For the ultra-fundamentalists, secular humanism, and the humanistic programs and curriculums it supposedly supports in the schools, is perceived as being anti-Christian and antifamily. According to Onalee McGraw, an educational consultant to the Heritage Foundation in Washington, D.C.:

> In the humanistic frame of reference, however, values are relative and ethics are situational. Children are therefore being taught at school that moral and social beliefs and behavior are not necessarily based on Judeo-Christian principles being taught by most families at home, but should be fashioned instead to suit the wishes and convenience of the majority or society as a whole.[25]

As the educational historian Diane Ravitch has pointed out, the New Right—and more specifically, in terms of the analysis of this book, the ultra-fundamentalists—have been successful when they have hit upon issues where there is a discontented public far larger than just themselves.[26] Ultra-fundamentalist critics have gained the attention of media and the general public, in part, because they have asked important questions about the public school system—questions that are concerned with How, What and Why we teach children. Ultimately the ultra-fundamentalists are asking what should be the nature and purpose of public education in a democratic society.

It is the belief of the author that an understanding of the ultra-fundamentalist position and how it effects public education is crucial for both educators and policy makers and for the public at large. In this book I will carefully examine the opinions, positions and philosophies expressed by ultra-fundamentalist leaders on and about public education in the United States. I will also explore the implications of their ideas and activities for public education in America.

Before beginning the main substance of this work it is important that the position of the author be clearly understood. As an educational historian and policy analyst I am concerned with the extent to which the various conservative Protestant religious groups (loosely associated with the fundamentalist movement and the "New Political Right") which I describe as ultra-fundamentalists, have distorted the history and role of the public schools in the development of American society and have put increasing pressure on American public education to conform exclusively to their philosophy and vision of education and culture. It is my belief that their efforts have produced tangible results, and that if they continue in their attempt to transform the American public school to fit their vision of education, they will in fact severely limit and weaken public education in the United States.

Finally, I wish to acknowledge the many people who have contributed to the research and writing of this book. James Ash, Arnold Cheyney,

Gilberto Cuevas and Robert Simpson of the University of Miami provided important sources and suggestions. Gary McCloskey, O.S.A. of Augustinian College, Washington, D.C. read this book in various drafts and provided excellent suggestions for its improvement. James Carper of Mississippi State University provided several helpful sources, as did Douglas Sloan of Teachers College, Columbia University. Asterie Baker Provenzo read through various drafts and provided thoughtful comments involving both substance and organization. Vivian Vieta—my undergraduate research assistant—spent dozens of hours finding materials and confirming citations. Her help was invaluable. Special thanks go to the staff of both the Heritage Foundation and People for the American Way for their assistance in undertaking the research for this book.

Chapter One

# Ultra-Fundamentalism and American Education

Fundamentalism began as a religious movement in the United States during the middle of the nineteenth century. An offshoot of Protestant "evangelicalism," American fundamentalism was a response to profound cultural changes in American society. Rapid industrialization and urbanization, new religious theories, the widespread acceptance of Darwin's theory of evolution and other changes influenced a radical redefinition of traditional values and institutions. For the fundamentalists, many of these changes were perceived as a direct attack upon the Bible. The forcers of Modernism posed a threat not only to their religious beliefs, but also to their vision of culture and society.[1]

While fundamentalism has manifested itself in many forms, it may be characterized as a movement within American "evangelical" Christianity which professes complete confidence in the literal interpretation of the Bible. It is preoccupied with the message of God's salvation of sinners through the death of Jesus Christ.[2]

By the 1920s, the Fundamentalists found themselves isolated from the mainstream of American life and culture. Their vision of traditional Protestant Christianity was decreasing in popularity.[3] The emerging American culture was passing them by. As the fundamentalist Joseph Wood Krutch observed at the time: "Both our practical morality and our emotional lives are adjusted to a world that no longer exists."[4]

The profound difference in outlook between the fundamentalists and mainstream American culture was revealed in the summer of 1925 when

1

William Jennings Bryan (representing the interests of antievolutionist and traditional Christians) argued against Clarence Darrow in the famous "Scopes Monkey Trial."[5] The Scopes trial had its origins in 1923 when several Southern states began passing laws that opposed the teaching of evolution in the public schools. The most famous of these laws was passed in 1925 in Tennessee. It was immediately challenged by John Scopes, a young biology teacher from Dayton, Tennessee. Although he was provided legal counsel by the American Civil Liberties Union, Scopes was found guilty of teaching evolution. Yet despite Scopes' conviction, national public sentiment was clearly in favor of the pro-evolutionary forces that Scopes represented. The trial has consistently been interpreted by historians as a defeat for the fundamentalist cause in the United States.[6]

According to this interpretation, the defeat of the fundamentalists at the Scopes trial represented the end of their influence as a religious and social force in American culture.[7] They were perceived as representing a continuation of the traditions of conservative nineteenth century American Protestant culture. Their humiliation at the trial was seen to reflect the passing of an older religious tradition in favor of a new scientific and technological order in America.

This interpretation has been put forward by a number of distinguished historians, the most important of whom is Richard Hofstadter. In his work *Anti-Intellectualism in American Life*, Holfstadter has argued that: "By the end of the century, it was painfully clear to fundamentalists that they were losing much of their influence and respectability." According to him, they wished: "to strike back at everything modern—the higher criticism, evolutionism, the social gospel, rational criticism of any kind."[8] Basing his interpretation largely on the work of William McLoughlin, Hofstadter argued that the fundamentalists' attack on evolution was an almost inevitable consequence of the social upheaval of the period immediately following the First World War.[9]

Hofstadter clearly underestimated the extent to which the fundamentalist movement was rooted in nineteenth century cultural traditions and, therefore, the ultimate strength of the movement. Subsequent scholars have argued that the roots of the movement and its opposition to Modernism lay much deeper than the cultural crisis of the 1920s. Ernest Sandeen, for example, recognized fundamentalism as a serious religious movement emerging in the United States during the middle of the nineteenth century.[10] While criticized by subsequent religious historians such as George F. Marsden for failing to sufficiently root fundamentalism in nineteenth century Protestant culture, Sandeen's emphasis on the integrity of the religious and intellectual aspects of fundamentalism was a valuable corrective to scholars such as Hofstader who had reduced fundamentalism largely to its social dimensions.

As Marsden has pointed out, had Hofstadter's, and in turn Sandeen's interpretation been correct, fundamentalism would not remain a significant force in American Protestantism today. When he published *Anti-Intellectualism in American Life* in 1962, Hofstadter assumed that the evolution controversy was long dead and buried. The recent court cases concerning evolution and creationism in California, Louisiana and Arkansas, as well as the textbook cases in Tennessee and Alabama, refute such an interpretation. As this book will attempot to demonstrate, fundamentalism has been and remains a powerful and influential force in American society. In areas such as public education it has, and will continue to have, a critical impact that cannot be ignored.

While their actual numbers are not known, the fundamentalist groups represent a significant segment of the general population.[11] Leaders within the movement claim that there are as many as 79 million "evangelical Christians" living in the United States. In a 1976 survey for the magazine *Christianity Today*, the pollster George Gallup reported that there were at least "fifty million Americans who claim to have had a born again experience."[12] Other scholars are more conservative in their numbers. George M. Marsden estimates that of roughly forty million evangelicals in the United States there are approximately four to five million—primarily dispensationalists and other strict separatists—who would describe themselves as fundamentalists.[13]

The ongoing influence of the fundamentalists as a social and political force can be seen beyond the public schools. Nowhere is this clearer than in the 1980 election. Conservative politicians of the New Right drew heavily on fundamentalist support in order to defeat prominent liberal politicans. The election campaigns of former United States Senators Dick Clark of Iowa, Wendall Anderson of Minnesota and Thomas McIntyre of New Hampshire were lost, in part, because of carefully organized opposition from conservative religious and political groups. Ronald Reagan's successful bid for the presidency certainly drew heavily on conservative Protestant and more specifically, fundamentalist support.

It is important to recognize that the fundamentalists are a diverse and complex group. As the religious scholar James Barr has argued, fundamentalism represents a set of religious beliefs that can be found in a wide-range of social and professional groups. Fundamentalism is by no means, as some have foolishly assumed, a preserve of the uneducated or the ignorant.[14] Instead, fundamentalism and in its more extreme manifestation, ultra-fundamentalism, represents a specific and coherent view of the world—one whose implications are of extraordinary importance to American education and culture.

## QUESTIONS POSED BY THE ULTRA-FUNDAMENTALISTS CONCERNING THE MEANING OF EDUCATION AND CULTURE

John Dewey in his work *Democracy and Education* argued that a community or social group maintains itself through a process of constant renewal in which the immature members of the group are educated. Through various agencies, unintentional and designed, a society transforms its youth into trustees of its resources and ideals. Education is thus a fostering, nurturing, and cultivating process.[15] In a democratic and pluralistic culture such as the United States, the question of what ideals and values are to be pursued as part of the educational system is a difficult one. "What should be taught?" This is among the most complicated and potentially controversial issues faced by contemporary educators.

Over the course of the past decade, the ultra-fundamentalists have emerged as an increasingly vocal and influential force in American education. In general, they have strongly opposed the current thrust of American public and private education. They have done so on the basis of what they believe are the underlying philosophical values and beliefs of our educational system. In doing so, they have also rejected the dominant moral and intellectual values of contemporary American culture and society.

The ultra-fundamentalists' attack on American education has proceeded along a number of different fronts. Textbooks and Curricula, Evolution versus Creationism, Sex Education and Prayer in the Public Schools are all issues that have been recently addressed by ultra-fundamentalist. Their attack has been both carefully planned and argued. As a result, the ultra-fundamentalists have emerged with a detailed and comprehensive critique of contemporary American schooling and culture.

Although this critique is one that many Americans may disagree with, it is, however, one that deserves careful attention and scrutiny. Part of the power of the ultra-fundamentalists' critique lies in the fact that they ask important questions such as: 1) What is the nature and purpose of our educational system? 2) What are the values and assumptions underlying our educational system? and, 3) How does the educational system meet the needs of not only the majority but also the minorities within our culture? Questions such as these deserve careful consideration. Before undertaking an analysis of the ultra-fundamentalists' current views concerning education, an examination of their understanding of the role education has played in the historical development of the United States is necessary.

## THE ULTRA-FUNDAMENTALIST'S INTERPRETATION OF AMERICAN EDUCATIONAL HISTORY

In their critique of contemporary American education the ultra-fundamentalists have constructed their own unique interpretation of the history of American education—one that is radically different from that of historians working within the mainstream of American educational history.

Recognizing the existence of an ultra-fundamentalist historiography of American education is more important than one may at first realize. Unlike groups of educational historians such as the Radical Revisionists, whose work is known almost exclusively in academic circles, the ideas and interpretations of Christian fundamentalist historians have made their way into the larger fundamentalist literature. Key to understanding the ultra-fundamentalists' interpretation of American educational history is the work of Rousas J. Rushdoony.

Rousas J. Rushdoony, a former missionary and ordained minister in the Orthodox Presbyterian Church, has contributed more than any other writer or scholar to the fundamentalist interpretation of American educational history. In works such as *The Messianic Character of American Education,* [16] and *Intellectual Schizophrenia: Culture, Crisis and Education,* [17] he has systematically analyzed, from an ultra-fundamentalist perspective, the work of such educational leaders as Horace Mann, James G. Carter, Nicholas Murray Butler, John Dewey, Edward Lee Thorndike, George Counts and Theodore Braemeld. He has also explored in detail the notion of "Education as Religion" and what he believes is the "Messianic" character of American education.

Rushdoony believes that there can be no compromise between "Calvinistic" (i.e. Christian/Religious) forms of education and that of "the Enlightenment and contemporary thought." Each is in total contradiction of the other. Beginning with the work of the English philosopher John Locke (1632-1704) there has been a tendency on the part of the modern state, through its educational system, to mold and shape the child for its own purposes. According to Rushdoony, the cosmopolitan nature of the modern state:

> is erosive and destructive of all aspects of culture except the monolithic state, which is then the ostensible creator and patron of culture. When it speaks of the whole child, it speaks of a passive creature who is to be molded by statist education for a concept of the good life radically divorced from God and from transcendental standards...[18]

Modern education by implication:

> is statist education, and the state is made the all embracing institution of which all other institutions are but facets. The state and the person, government and individual, become thus the two realities of such a worldview. Both demand freedom and power for themselves. The state

recognizes no law beyond itself and the individual insists on his own autonomy and intimacy.[19]

Citing Calvinistic thinkers such as Kuyper, Bavinck and C. Van Til, Rushdoony argues that any system of education must begin with "biblical revelation and the ontological trinity."[20] The self-realization of the individual is to the advantage of all and is "advanced by and integral with the self-realization of others."[21] In the statist system, the fulfillment and self-realization of the individual are at the expense of others and may in fact even involve their sacrifice.[22] For ultra-fundamentalists such as Rushdoony, knowledge is not merely a collection of data, it is:

> data seen in relationship to God as the sovereign and almighty one. Knowledge comes from God; it is the reverential subordination of all knowing to the Creator. Man cannot identify himself in terms of himself, nor, ultimately can he sustain any knowledge in terms of himself. Autonomous man must know everything or he knows nothing if he be consistent to his principle. The idea of exhaustive knowledge claims far more than biblical revelation, which definitely does not assert itself to be exhaustive. The biblical revelation, however, definitely undergirds all reality.[23]

Unless placed in the context of biblical revelation, knowledge by itself "tends to disintegrate, and to be prostituted."[24]

Rushdoony believes that the movement towards statist education has its origins in Antiquity and the Renaissance. It gained impetus, however, with the Common School Movement and the work of the educational leaders Horace Mann and James G. Carter. Arguing that the control of education determines the future direction of a culture, Rushdoony explains that:

> Control of children and their education is control of the future. Humanists have always understood this. Horace Mann, James G. Carter, and their many associates (including Senator Charles Sumner), were all Unitarians; they hated the Puritan faith of their forefathers with a passion. Their purpose in promoting state control of education was twofold. *First*, they rightfully understood that the only way to destroy Biblical faith was to control the schools and, little by little, remove Christianity and introduce Humanism. *Second*, they were Centralists or statist, men who believed that salvation comes by work of statist legislation or law.[25]

A century and a half later, instead of Horace Mann's Millennium,

Rushdoony argues that we have arrived at a social and moral breakdown of our culture. As he explains:

> The messianic character of education has not changed; it has only expanded in its scope, and accordingly, it claims to support financial and intellectual. Sex education, counseling, psychological testing, psychiatric aid, all these things are added in the abiding conviction that knowledge is not only power but moral virtue. Given these things and more, it is asserted the new society will be created. Meanwhile social disintegration grows more rapidly, for the doctrine of the universal human rights ends in the mutual cancellation of rights to the mass man, to the state. Democracy always perished from an overdose of democracy. Standards perish before majority rule; the group morale outweighs morality; the insistence on rights nullifies the doctrine of responsibility.[26]

Rushdoony does not deny what he believes to have been either Mann's sincerity or Mann's belief that he was a true Christian. He does, however, believe that by interpreting Christianity as freedom, and education as salvation, Mann undercut both Christianity and the republic.[27]

Whether Rushdoony is dealing with Horace Mann, G. Stanley Hall, or John Dewey, the same themes repeat themselves over and over again: the abandonment of eternal verities or truth and the development of a statist system of education which emphasizes the needs of society rather than the needs of the individual. As he explains near the conclusion of *The Messianic Character of American Education:*

> Statist education increasingly assumes that (1) the child is the child of the state or the property of the state, which can therefore interfere extensively with parental authority. (2) The state "priesthood" of educators are best able to rear the child and prepare him for life, viewed as statist life. (3) Statist education is alone "objective" and hence true, the state having the impartiality and transcendence of a god. Statist education is thus entrance into the true catholicity of the civil religion of the modern state.[28]

John Dewey is seen as having abandoned religious thought and convictions in favor of an instrumental or pragmatic point of view—a "scientific philosophy"—which had no room for *a priori* assumptions, metaphysical beliefs, purely religious presuppositions or eternal truth.[29] Yet, according to Rushdoony, Dewey's philosophical system implies a metaphysical point of view. As he explains:

> An avowed metaphysics is an open and vulnerable metaphysics. But a metaphysics can be presupposed and veiled behind a facade of prag-

matism, and an implicit metaphysics is no less a metaphysics. Dewey, the pragmatic, was more firmly wedded to eternal verities than many a metaphysician, and his theory, based on an implicit and unreasoning dogmatism, unleashed a new Islam into American education and philosophy, savagely intolerant, belligerently contemptuous of all previous learning and thought, and dedicated to an educational jargon unfamiliar and irrational to all who were not devotees of this new Mohammed.[30]

According to Rushdoony, Dewey's work is based upon a number of presuppositions or axioms: 1) that as an Hegelian, Dewey accepted the concept of "continuity." Dualisms of any sort are false; and 2) that "growth" (physical, intellectual and moral) is an exemplification of the principle of continuity. Because of his belief in continuity and growth, Rushdoony goes on to argue that Dewey's philosophical system assumed a faith in the process of "change."[31] At the heart of Rushdoony's argument is his belief that Dewey's philosophy is based on a series of highly specific presuppositions or axioms—ones that Dewey had to assume on the basis of faith.

Rushdoony's significance as the leading fundamentalist interpreter of American educational history lies in his influence on other more popular authors. In work after work by leading ultra-fundamentalist such as Tim LaHaye, Barbara Morris, Alan N. Grover, Henry M. Morris and Homer Duncan, direct or indirect reference can be found to Rushdoony's work. In fact, one can argue that the most of what is written by ultra-fundamentalists concerning the historical development of American education is either a gloss taken directly from Rushdoony's work, or a repetition of his arguments against a statist system of education placed in a more specific context. The extent to which this is true can be seen by a brief review of some of the more popular contemporary ultra-fundamentalist writers on education.


## CONTEMPORARY ULTRA-FUNDAMENTALIST
## WRITERS ON EDUCATION

Among the most vocal of the ultra-fundamentalist critics of American education is Barbara Morris. Morris, who is the founder of the *Barbara M. Morris Report* and a staff correspondent of the *National Educator* is the author of *Change Agents in the Schools*.[32] Like Rushdoony, she believes that public schools are destructive for the children who attend them and that they are ultimately betraying us as a nation. According to Morris:

"The best thing that could happen to education in America would be the demise of government schools...."[33]

Morris's work has received the endorsement of groups such as the John Birch society, which has described her book *Change Agents in the Schools* as a:

> dynamite book which shows how government schools, sneaky educators, humanism, and values education combine to mold our government and our youngsters.[34]

She has summarized what she believes to be the real educational issues that concern religious conservatives such as herself. Most focus around the statist issues outlined by Rushdoony. These include:

1. the promotion of articles of faith put forward in documents such as the *Humanist Manifesto II*;
2. the usurpation of parental rights and prerogatives by the educational system;
3. the invasion of personal privacy through the use of techniques such as values clarification and behavioral modification;
4. the failure to convey traditional knowledge and information—specifically basic skills;
5. the preparation of teachers to act as agents of social, political and economic change; and
6. the use of traditional subject areas as a means of promoting "humanistic goals."[35]

Morris's objections focus on contemporary American education. Yet her critique clearly has its foundations—consciously or unconsciously—in issues that extend back to the founding of the American public school system and the work of educational leaders such as Horace Mann. Other ultra-fundamentalist writers are more specific in their use of historical interpretations as the basis for their discussions of the current condition of American education. Tim LaHaye, for example, has argued in his book *The Battle for the Mind* that Mann was in large part responsible for the "humanization" and secularization of American culture. As LaHaye explains:

> The process did not begin with Horace Mann, although he probably did more to humanize American education in the nineteenth century than any other educator, and thus we tend to trace humanistic roots back to him. Mann was vigorously opposed by ministers of his day, who foresaw

the shift from a biblical to a humanistic base for education, but their resistance was gradually overcome.[36]

Henry Morris, a colleague of LaHaye's at Christian Heritage College has argued in a similar context that Mann believed

> in the uniscriptural doctrine of the natural goodness of man, so that universal state-compelled education would, in his view, ultimately develop a perfect society. He stressed that every man had a basic right to a full education, to help him reach the highest potential of his innate abilities, and that since the Christian schools were not meeting this need, the state should do it. The state should furthermore, prepare its teachers—through its "normal" schools—so that they in turn could prepare each new generation for optimum service to society.[37]

For LaHaye, Mann's influence, although important, was nothing when compared with that of John Dewey. According to LaHaye, Dewey viewed traditional education with alarm. In rejecting traditionalism Dewey instead proposed:

1. Expression, and cultivation of individuality (as opposed to imposition from above).
2. Free activity (as opposed to external discipline).
3. Learning through experience (as opposed to texts and teachers).
4. Acquiring skills as a means of attaining ends which have direct vital appeal (as opposed to drill).
5. Making the most of the opportunities of the present life (as opposed to preparation for a more-or-less remote future).
6. Acquaintance with a changing world (as opposed to static aims and materials).[38]

According to LaHaye, allowing principles such as these to be pursued by the Humanists has been largely responsible for the current crisis in education and contemporary culture. Free development of oneself has led to selfishness and rebellion on the part of many individuals. Learning through experience—the foundation of Dewey's experimental educational philosophy—means that one is limited to only one's observations and experience. The wisdom of "history, learned teachers, and Scripture" are ignored. By focusing on the present rather than the hereafter, we are distracted from the fact that our life in this world is simply a preparation for eternity. Finally, learning to cope with a changing world, has the effect of denying the idea that there are absolute truths or "eternal verities."

There are a number of ironies to be found in the ultra-fundamentalist critique of American educational history. In their opposition to state control or statist education, they manifest opinions that in some respects closely parallel those of the Revisionist and Radical Revisionist historians of American education.[39] Like the Revisionists' historiography, the ultra-fundamentalists develop an interpretation that rejects the notion of "the public school triumphant." Similarly, they challenge the belief that universal schooling and innovations such as the Progressive Education Movement have been of benefit to American culture and society.

In the ultra-fundamentalist historigraphy of American education, the schools are considered to be value laiden institutions, which ultimately perpetuate the values and beliefs of the state. Such an interpretation merits careful reflection and consideration.

In the following chapters I will attempt to outline major areas of concern articulated by ultra-fundamentalists. Chapter Two, "Censorship and the Ultra-Fundamentalists" examines book banning and censorship efforts by ultra-fundamentalist groups since the mid-1970s. Chapter Three, "Textbooks and the Curriculum" examines the ultra-fundamentalists' increasing censorship of instructional materials and some of the major educational protests they have been involved with in recent years. Chapter Four, "Creationism and the Schools," examines the debate of Creation versus Evolution in the public schools and how the ultra-fundamentalists have advocated their own theologically based interpretation of biology and the sciences. Chapter Five, "The Family and Education," introduces the ultra-fundamentalists' belief that the power and authority of the traditional family is being undermined through secular oriented educational programs in the public schools. Chapter Six, "School Prayer and State Regulation of Christian Schools," looks at the issue of school prayer and the ultra-fundamentalist crusade to reinstate mandatory prayer in the public schools, as well as objections voiced by the ultra-fundamentalists concerning state regulation of Christian schools. Chapter Seven, "Implications of the Ultra-Fundamentalist Critique of American Education," concludes the book with an examination of the significance and meaning of the ultra-fundamentalist critique for public education in the United States.

# Chapter Two

# *Censorship and the*
# *Ultra-Fundamentalists*

---

In their battle for the public schools, the ultra-fundamentalists have used a number of methods to bring attention to their cause. Nowhere have they been as effective as in their use of censorship. The struggle over censorship, which has been going on since the middle of the 1970s, is not just a simple confrontation between conservative and liberal forces in American society. As Stephen Arons has eloquently argued:

> censorship is in fact a highly complex set of reactions to the faulty design of America's school systems. Beneath the surface of what is often described as the struggle of the narrow-minded against the open-minded, families are taking seriously the 100-year old ideology of compulsory schooling: that to be concerned with the education of one's own children is human but to be concerned with the education of everyone else's children is divine.[1]

According to Arons:

> Censorship is more than just censorship. It is a battle over the transmission of culture required by a system that prescribes majority control of education decisions for all but the wealthy.[2]

If the rhetoric used by ultra-fundamentalist writers is any indicator, then they see themselves as not only being engaged in a battle for the minds and souls of their children, but also in a battle over the definition of American culture and society. As Onalee McGraw explains:

> Can there be any doubt that the past decade has generated the most pervasive and widespread dissatisfaction with the present state-supported school system since its establishment? The public no longer accepts the premise that the state school, in addition to the home and the church, is the best vehicle through which American children must be socialized to be adjusted and productive participants in the "American way of life."[3]

The ultra-fundamentalists have consciously rejected the public school as an agent of enlightenment and social reform. Instead, they see it as a negative manifestation of an increasingly secularized society.

This rejection of public education and schooling on the part of the ultra-fundamentalists is of much greater consequence than most people realize. The success of American public schooling, throughout its history has depended upon a reasonable consensus within local communities as to what the aims and purposes of education should be. Without such a consensus the public schools ultimately cannot function.

Historically, many groups have been excluded from participating in determining what went on in the schools their children attended because of their race, ethnicity, religion or gender. With the passage of legislation such as the 1964 Civil Rights Act, the consensus traditionally found within most communities has become more and more strained, more and more fragile.

When the ultra-fundamentalists talk about the threat of secular humanism, they are probably more often than not, responding to very real social forces that are redefining American society. Viet Nam, the Woman's Movement, the Civil Rights Movement, the massive growth of media and telecommunications, the increasingly widespread acceptance and use of drugs, changing demographic patterns affecting the traditional family, and diverse economic pressures have radically redefined American society since the early 1960s.

Stephen Arons has argued that the modern censorship controversy, with the intense emotions and social polarization it generates, may in fact be "the modern equivalent of the war over state religions fought in seventeenth and eighteenth centuries."[4] It is at the very least, a conflict between opposing ideologies—opposing ways of raising children and of understanding the world in which we live. It is in this context that the ultra-fundamentalist critique of American public schooling must be understood. The struggle over textbooks and other reading materials, as well as schooling in general:

is, among other things, an attempt to impose meaning on social order and, in the process, to define personal identity. The myriad of petty struggles to condone or condemn books used in classroom and library are reactions to the alienating confusions of a culture in which customary explanations no longer seem to have the power to explain very much.[5]

The ultra-fundamentalist conflict over censorship and the curriculum is about the meaning of American culture, the changes that we have experienced in recent decades, and the possibilities that we as a people possess in terms of the future.

## LOCAL CENSORSHIP EFFORTS
## AS PART OF A NATIONAL MOVEMENT

Edward B. Jenkinson, Professor of English Education at Indiana University and Chairman of the National Council of English Teachers Committee Against Censorship, has written extensively about the impact of the ultra-fundamentalists on the censorship of school textbooks and library materials.[6] Jenkinson first began his research on censorship in the early 1970s. At that time, he assumed that most censorship efforts involved individual parents acting by themselves to protest about a book or set of curriculum materials they did not want their children to read. According to Jenkinson, however, this was not the case:

I soon learned that my assumption, based on my own experiences as a classroom teacher in the fifties and as a college instructor working with teachers in the sixties, was open to challenge. Individual parents still protest books, but many of them today do so with the advice of one or more of at least two hundred organizations in this nation that want to change the public schools. [7]

Since 1979, when Jenkinson published the above quote, he has concluded that there probably are in fact no less than 2,000 national, state, and local organizations involved in protesting textbooks and other curricular materials. Among these are both liberal and conservative critics ranging from the National Association for the Advancement of Colored People to the Ku Klux Klan. Among the most prominent of the ultra-fundamentalist groups at the national level are America's Future, Billy James Hargis' Christian Crusade, The John Birch Society, the Christian Anti-Communism Crusade, the Creation-Science Research Center, the Eagle Forum, Educational Research Analysts and the Heritage Foundation.[8]

Numerous ultra-fundamentalist groups and books provide information to their supporters on how to organize parent and community protest
groups. In Ethel Herr's *Schools: How Parents Can Make a Difference,* for
example, a two page appendix is included on how to organize a parent
protest group.[9] Connaught Marsher in her book *Blackboard Tyranny*
provides detailed suggestions on how to organize a systematic "letters to
the editor" campaign. In her instructions she emphasizes that:

> The crucial thing here is not to give the *appearance* of an organized
> campaign. Personally ask different 'reliables' in your club to write a letter
> to the editor on a specific day on a specific set of the topics at issue.[10]

In a similar vein Marsher goes on to suggest that if one appears on a radio
or television talk show it is a good strategy to have your friends call in to
ask questions and make favorable comments to support the position that
you are taking.[11]

Mel and Norma Gabler, the most effective of the ultra-fundamentalist
censors, provide very specific instructions on "Mounting the Offensive
Against Undesirable Texts" in "A Parents Guide to Textbook Review and
Reform," published by the Heritage Foundation. Seven specific suggestions are given to parents interested in "reforming" the curriculum in their
local schools. These include:

1.  learning about textbook adoption procedures in your state and local
    school district,
2.  becoming thoroughly familiar with the textbooks that you are
    objecting to,
3.  marking the objectionable passages of the books,
4.  holding your best evidence in reserve when testifying before an
    educational body,
5.  staying on the offensive,
6.  don't hold expectations of easy victories, and
7.  work in groups.[12]

The Gablers go on to suggest that they, and other groups such as
America's Future, can be contacted for reviews of textbooks. As they
explain:

> Countless hours of work on your part may be saved if there is a review of
> the book in question already available. We have thousands of textbook
> reviews, our own and those sent to us from many other states. Most of the

reviews are by page, paragraph and line, prepared by parents and for parents, and done with consideration for the age and knowledge level of the student.[13]

In dealing with local schol systems they suggest that to maximize one's effectiveness one should:

cultivate a friendly, continuing relationship with board members and candidates for the board. Remember, basic education is "in" now. The standard National Educational Association line that parents who object to recent educational trends are "right wing extremists" has a very hollow ring today. The failure of a decade of expensive "innovations" to improve education and the continuous decline in academic achievement has been widely reported in the popular media.[14]

Printed materials are often provided by ultra-fundamentalist groups at the national level to help individuals with local school book protests. In 1984, over six years after the passage of the "Hatch Amendment" (20 U.S.C. 1232h), which requires that parental permission must be obtained before children can be involved in federally funded experimental teaching programs or psychological research, the Eagle Forum began to circulate a form letter which could be used across the country "for filing complaints first at the local level, and then with the U.S. Department of Education."[15] Specifically, the form letter which is addressed to the "School Board President," states that:

Under U.S. legislation and court decisions, parents have the primary responsibility for their children's education, and pupils have certain rights which the schools may not deny. Parents have the right to assure that their children's beliefs and moral values are not undermined by the schools. Pupils have the right to have and to hold their values and moral standards without direct or indirect manipulation by the schools through curricula, textbooks, audio-visual materials, or supplementary assignments.[16]

The letter then requests that the writer's child not be involved in any psychological exams or treatments, values clarification courses, programs in death education (including abortion, euthanasia, suicide, etc.), drug and alcohol education, sex education, guided fantasy techniques, discussions of witchcraft, occultism, the supernatural and Eastern mysticism, political affiliations and beliefs of students and their families, personal religious beliefs and practices, as well as a whole range of other topics, unless these materials have been reviewed by the author of the letter and written consent given for their use. Specific reference is then made in the letter to the legal requirements of the Hatch Amendment.[17]

Significantly, when Orin Hatch, author of the Hatch Amendment, discovered that his legislation was being used as a blanket regulation to block instruction in the public schools, he made it very clear that the purpose of the amendment was "to guarantee the rights of parents to have their children excused from federally funded activities under carefully specified circumstances."[18] According to Hatch, these activities were "non-scholastic in nature."[19]

The improper use of the Hatch Amendment has allowed local censors to limit virtually any kind of classroom discussion. Open-ended questions almost automatically become subject to controversy. By definition the curriculum becomes limited to strictly factual presentations, subject to neither interpretation or discussion.

## CENSORSHIP AS VIEWED BY THE
## ULTRA-FUNDAMENTALISTS

Onalee McGraw, writing in a recent Heritage Foundation publication, has argued that censorship has been represented in the popular media as something that has been imposed by the conservative right. She maintains that instead, censorship has been a major part of the attempt of "feminists and other liberal groups to influence textbook and library selections."[20] According to McGraw, major publishers have submitted to the demands of feminist and liberal pressure groups concerning the content of textbooks, while ignoring the complaints of more conservative groups about the political and sociological content of the books which they publish.[21]

At the center of the censorship issue is the question of what values should be promoted by the educational system. Ultra-fundamentalist leaders clearly see their attempts to limit what is used in the schools as a crusade involving the defense of personal privacy and the rights of parents. Censorship activities lead by conservative religious groups have been on the upswing in recent years. A 1982 survey of high school librarians reported that during the five previous years the number of respondents who reported an increase in censorship activities within their schools had increased from 1 percent to 17 percent.[22] During the 1984-85 school year, People for the American Way documented censorship incidents in forty-six of the fifty states. More than 42 percent of the challenges led to the removal of materials from schools.[23] Compared to the 1982-1983 period, the number of censorship challenges increased 66.6 percent in 1984-85.[24]

According to the American Library Association, during the 1979-1980 school year, one-fourth of all school administrators and librarians in the United States reported challenges to various materials used in their schools and libraries. Among materials that were objected to included: *The Diary of Anne Frank, The American Heritage Dictionary, Newsweek, Slaughterhouse Five, The Catcher in the Rye,* and *Ladies Home Journal.*[25]

In their publication *Attacks on the Freedom to Learn: A 1984-1985 Report,* People for the American Way outline in detail the works that were most often attacked by censors across the country. According to their research, Judy Blume's *Deenie, Blubber, Tiger Eyes,* and *Then Again, Maybe I Won't,* J.D. Salinger's *The Catcher in the Rye,* Robert Cormier's *The Chocolate War,* John Steinbeck's *Of Mice and Men* and Franco Zeffirelli's film "Romeo and Juliet" were the materials most frequently responsible for causing protests at the local level during the 1984-1985 school year.[26]

In Peoria, Illinois, for example, there was opposition to including Judy Blume's *Deenie, Blubber,* and *Then Again, Maybe I Won't* in the Peoria School District's elementary libraries because of their "sexual content," "strong language" and "lack of social or literary value." Two school committees made up of school personnel recommended the removal of the books. The school board, however, returned the books to the library shelves limiting access to them to older students, or students with parental consent.[27]

In a 1983-1984 survey of public, academic and school libraries in Delaware, J.D. Salinger's *The Catcher in the Rye* was described as the "dirtiest book ever written."[28] In Cornwall High School in New York Robert Cormier's novel *The Chocolate War* and *I am the Cheese* were objected to as "humanistic," "destroying religious and moral beliefs and national spirit." While comments and discussion were heard by the local school board, no specific action was taken against the books.[29] At Nampa High School near Boise, Idaho, John Steinbeck's *Of Mice and Men* was objected to by parents because of its "inappropriateness."[30] Finally, objections to the film "Romeo and Juliet" were made by parents at Troy High School in Troy, New York who objected to scenes in which "partially nude" characters appeared.[31]

Certainly not all of these protests have been instigated by ultra-fundamentalists. According to People for the American Way, 24.1 percent of the censorship incidents reported were initiated by organized censorship groups aligned with ultra-fundamentalist organizations such as the Eagle Forum, the Moral Majority, the Pro-Family Forum and Educational Research Analysts. Only 12 percent of the protests were initiated by school personnel, while the remaining approximately 65 percent were led by legislators, preachers and individual parents. According to People for the American Way, the majority of the complaints lodged by this latter group closely paralleled the objections consistently raised by far right censorship groups.[32]

Censorship incidents are undoubtedly intimidating for local school and library officials, whether such protests are instigated by individuals or organized groups. Most are resolved at a local level and receive little or no national attention. In the following section we look at four recent and well publicized incidents involving ultra-fundamentalists and censorship issues will provide an understanding of the major issues at work.

*Kanawha County and the Battle for the Books*

The contemporary controversy over ultra-fundamentalism and censorship has its origins in the 1974 Kanawha County, West Virginia "battle of the books." Early in 1974 a group of five public school teachers submitted a list of language arts textbooks to the school district's board of education which were to be used in the public schools. On April 11, 1974 the books were approved by the board, but their purchase was delayed until their content passed a final process of review.

The request to review the texts before they were purchased came from Alice Moore, a member of the school board and the wife of a local conservative, self-ordained Protestant minister. After careful review, Moore objected to a number of the books that were selected for the language arts program on the basis that they were in her opinion:

> disrespectful of authority and religion, destructive of social and cultural values, obscene, pornographic, unpatriotic, or in violation of individual and familial rights of privacy.[33]

Commenting on three of the books that she found particularly objectionable, Moore explained that:

> The more I read, the more I was shocked. They were full of negative references to Christianity and God. There was lots of profanity and anti-American and racist antiwhite stories. They presented a warped viewpoint of life, as if every black carried a knife, was locked into a slum, and was made to look inferior.[34]

The books that were recommended for use in the Kanawha schools were requested by the teachers in order to meet the requirements of a multicultural and multi-ethnic mandate outlined in a 1970 state law.[35]

They included literary materials depicting urban life and culture—some of them controversial in nature.

In the month between the April and May school board meetings, Moore contacted Mel and Norma Gabler. She had learned about the Gablers through the educational review group America's Future. They were reviewing a number of the books included on the list that had been recommended in Kanawha County, and they agreed to send Moore supporting material and reviews.[36]

At a special school board meeting held on May 16th, the textbook selection committee explained how the recommended books were to be used in the curriculum. Moore argued that the content of some of the books as well as their general underlying philosophy was inappropriate. At a May 24th meeting, ten local ministers spoke in favor of the recommended books. At a meeting two days later, twenty-seven opposing ministers described the recommended books as being indecent and immoral. At a meeting held June 27th, which was attended by nearly a thousand people, the school board voted three to two to drop eight of the most controversial textbooks from the recommended list.[37]

The battle had only just begun. Moore had won a partial victory with the withdrawal of eight books from the recommended list. During the first week of school in September textbook protestors kept a total of eight thousand children out of school (in a district of approximately 46,000 students). More than four thousand coal miners stayed away from work. Pickets closed bus depots, grocery stores and construction sites. The windows in the board of education building in Charleston were blown out by gunfire.[38] On September 11th, the school board announced that all of the adopted textbooks would be submitted to a citizen's committee for review. On September 12th students at George Washington High School staged a "walk out" in order to protest the removal of controversial English textbooks for a thirty day period.[39]

The various protests had a significant impact on the local community. Local coal companies estimated that they lost two million dollars because of the strike. Damage to the schools cost hundreds of thousands of dollars.[40] On September 14th a truck driver was shot and wounded in conjunction with the protests. On the 15th another man was shot and a second one beaten. Kanawha County teachers voted against a one day sick-out protesting the board's decision to have the textbooks reviewed by a committee of citizens. While sentiment for the sick-out seems to have been strong, there was a feeling that it would rekindle violence in the community.[41]

The various interpretations of the Kanawha County textbook controversy are extremely interesting. James C. Hefley, in his book *Are*

*Textbooks Harming Your Children?* explains that:

> The national media carried stories that poorly educated fundamentalist,
> rural, coal-mining "creekers" were protesting schoolbooks in opposition
> to better educated professional and business people in Charleston who
> wanted the books to remain in the schools. It was ignorance against
> enlightenment, stubborn dogmatism against progress, prejudice against
> tolerance, censorship against democracy. Some reports said protestors
> were racially motivated and did not want minority representations in
> texts. Others allowed that the protests might stem from a sense of
> frustrated powerlessness to stop the destruction of values of another
> era.[42]

Hefley argues that the reality of the situation was in fact quite different.

According to his account of the "The Truth About West Virginia" (the
title of his chapter in *Are Textbooks Harming Your Children?*), Moore
and her supporters were simply exercising their democratic right to
determine the content of what their children were taught in the schools.[43]

In fact, the evidence seems to suggest that some of the conservative
forces in the community were seriously overstepping the boundaries of
acceptable behavior. On September 16th it was necessary to temporarily
close the schools. While they were opened again on the seventeenth,
inflammatory statements continued to fuel the fire of controversy. On
September thirtieth, for example, the Reverend Charles Quigley asked for
prayers for the death of the three school board members who supported
the adoption of the textbooks.

> I am asking Christian people to pray that God will kill the giants that have
> mocked and made fun of dumb fundamentalists.[44]

During October and November parents and a minister were arrested for
trying to keep school buses from leaving a garage. Eleven mines were
closed. School buses were vandalized. Molotov cocktails (gasoline bombs)
were thrown at a local elementary school. A car belonging to a parent who
had been arrested for picketing was blown up. Two school buses were hit
by shot gun blasts. A car belonging to parents who sent their children to
school during the protest was fire-bombed, and a state police car escorting
a school bus with children in it was hit by sniper fire.[45]

Early in October Mel and Norma Gabler, at the invitation of Alice
Moore, flew to Charleston to speak to groups throughout the area—each
speaking separately to several different groups a day. They stayed for a
total of six days. James Hefley recounts that:

While in West Virginia, Mel and Norma learned firsthand about the arrogance of the Charleston press toward the protestors. One of the papers asked them to come in for an interview. They arrived to face a young man sitting behind a typewriter with his feet on the desk. He never stood up, but merely indicated that she and Mel take seats across the room. He asked a question and when Norma started across the room to show him a book, he held up his hands. "Hey, hey, I feel as if I am being attacked," he said mockingly.[46]

Evidence would suggest that a real clash of cultures was at work in the Kanawaha County controversy. Robert M. O'Neil has argued that a number of causal factors were unusual if not unique to the situation. These included the merger into a single school district of people with totally disparate points of view. As part of the consolidation of the school district, "creekers" (the rural residents of the county) and the city residents were forced to attend the same schools. Tensions developed with the introduction of new and nontraditional curriculum materials. In addition, the strong tradition of independence and protest that had developed around the coal mines probably contributed significantly to the level of controversy.[47]

On November 8, 1974, the school board voted four to one to return all of the controversial textbooks to the schools with the exception of the D.C. Heath *Communicating* series and the level four text of Houghton Mifflin's *Interaction* series.[48] On November 21, 1974, the Board of Education of Kanawaha County presented a set of guidelines for textbook selection. These included:

1. that textbooks recognize the sanctity of the home and not intrude upon the privacy of the family;
2. that textbooks not contain profanity;
3. that textbooks respect the rights of ethnic, religious and racial groups;
4. that textbooks not encourage or promote racial hatred;
5. that textbooks encourage loyalty to the United States;
6. that textbooks teach the true history of the United States; and
7. that textbooks used in the study of English emphasize traditional rules of grammar, etc.[49]

A screening procedure was also set up for the review of textbooks. Three parents and one teacher were assigned to each subject area and a vote of 75 percent of the committee was required to retain any textbook.[50]

The National Education Association established an Inquiry Panel to review the textbook controversy in Kanawha County. It concluded that the guidelines and procedures adopted by the school system made it possible for the protestors to impose their values on the schools and the community. According to the N.E.A. report:

> There are many aspects of the textbook adoption procedures that will make the selection and adoption of instructional procedures a nearly impossible task—and a nightmare. The process can only flounder amidst a welter of committees, teams and councils that have been created. Under the new system, the influence of lay citizens is not only present, it literally permeates every area of curriculum planning and textbook evaluation.[51]

By the time texts worked their way through the system of outside review, the selection of materials left to choose from "may have been so narrowed as to make a mockery of the selection process."[52]

## *Warsaw, Indiana: Book Burning in the Heartland*

The Kanawha County textbook controversy was the first of many such protests in the past ten years that have pitted the values of ultra-fundamentalist groups against local school districts. During the summer of 1977, the board of education for the Warsaw, Indiana schools banned the use of Sidney Simon's textbook *Values Clarification*, which had been used in an elective high school course for the past two years. The banning of the book, which was in direct violation of written policy requiring a review committee and a superintendent's recommendation for the removal of library or instructional material, was accomplished by a school board motion that called for the book to be "thrown out, removed, banned, destroyed, and forbidden to be used."[53]

On August 25th, once again in violation of its procedures, the board unanimously ordered the discontinuation of elective courses in Black Literature, Gothic Literature, Science Fiction, Folklore and Legends, and Whatever Happened to Mankind? At the beginning of the fall term Teresa Burneau, an English teacher who taught a course on Women in Literature was told by her principal that she could not use two books included on her reading list, *The Stepford Wives* and *Growing Up Female*, because they might be offensive to certain members of the community. In October, the principal instructed Ms. Burneau not to use *Go Ask Alice*—the anonymous diary of a teenage drug addict. By Thanksgiving Ms. Burneau was told that she could not use Sylvia Plath's book of poems *The Bell Jar* in her class.[54]

The books used by Ms. Burneau were seen as being objectionable because they raised issues such as suicide, divorce, adultery and drug addiction and in some instances used profane language. On December 15, 1977 the Warsaw Senior Citizen's Club burned forty copies of Simon's book *Values Clarification*. On April 17, 1978 three teachers, including Teresa Burneau and Joan Dupont, secretary of the Warsaw Teacher's Union, and an outspoken critic of the censorship activities in the school district, were fired.

Charges of unfair labor practices were brought by the teachers union against the school district and hearings were eventually held by the Indiana Employment Relations Board. In the spring of 1979 four suits were filed in federal district court of Indiana challenging that censorship had taken place in the Warsaw schools. In *Zykan v. Warsaw Community School Corporation* a class action suit asked for the restoration of the books and courses that had been eliminated. The basis of the suit was whether or not a school board has the right to remove books and courses, as well as fire teachers because they are not in agreement with the social and political values held by the board.[55]

*Zykan v. Warsaw* was dismissed in 1979 by a federal district court for failing to state a constitutional claim. A 1980 appeal to the federal circuit court laid the groundwork for a trial demonstrating that the Warsaw school board had acted to impose antifeminist values on the plaintiffs. By that time the Zykan family, who had originally filed the suit, had left the area. Teresa Burneau had accepted a small financial settlement from the school system and had moved to Washington. Resources were limited and the case was dismissed with the consent of the civil liberties lawyer.[56] As had been the case in Kanawha County, conservative forces had once again predominated.

Stephen Arons indicates that in conversations he had with Warsaw residents the question of authority was the central issue in both the censorship controversy and their lives in general:

> authority of men over women, of fundamentalism over secular human-ism, of the school board over the teachers, of the family over the school board, and of parents over children.[57]

Ultimately, the citizens of Warsaw felt that their value system was being seriously threatened. In order to preserve these values they were willing to allow books to be censored, obstruct the legal process and destroy the careers of teachers.

## *Board of Education, Island Trees Free School v. Pico*

Neither the censorship controversies in Kanawha County or Warsaw, Indiana made their way to the Supreme Court. In *Board of Education,*

*Island Trees Free School* v. *Pico* five high school students sued their local school board for removing nine books from its library including: Bernard Malamud's *The Fixer*, Kurt Vonnegut's *Slaughterhouse Five*, the anonymous *Go Ask Alice*, Eldridge Cleaver's *Soul on Ice, A Reader for Writers*, edited by Jerome Archer, Alice Childress's *A Hero Ain't Nothing But a Sandwich*, Piri Thomas's portrayal of Puerto Rican street life in New York City *Down These Mean Streets*, *The Naked Ape* by Desmond Morris and *Best Stories by Negro Writers*, edited by Langston Hughes.[58]

The case began in September 1975 when three members of the school board attended a conference sponsored by a conservative right-wing group called Parents of New York-United. A list of "objectionable" books was circulated at the meeting which included eleven titles listed in the school system's library. The board members ordered that all eleven titles be removed from the library. Eventually two titles were restored.[59] Protest to the removal of the books was immediate. Rather than mount a political campaign against the board members responsible for censoring the library's books, a group of students led by the high school student council president Steven Pico sued the board, claiming that their first amendment rights had been violated. A lower court dismissed the case, another appeal was undertaken and eventually the case made its way to the Supreme Court.[60]

Six years later in 1981 the Supreme Court ruled that the books banned by the Island Pines school board could not be removed from the school's library because of their "anti-American content." If removal were to occur, it would have to be because they violated obscenity laws. On August 12, 1981, after being advised to do so by its lawyer and receiving a petition from 1,200 parents in the community, the Island Trees school board voted to return all nine books to the library.[61]

Because of the way the case was presented to the Supreme Court, *Board of Education, Island Trees Free Schools* v. *Pico* did not provide a clear or decisive interpretation concerning the censorship issue. In the censorship cases in Kanawha County, Warsaw, Indiana and Island Trees, Long Island, censorship of reading materials and textbooks was resulting from the actions of ultra-fundamentalists. This situation was recently reversed in a widely publicized incident in Hawkins, Tennessee where fundamentalist students were required to participate in a public school elementary reading program.

### *Mozert v. Hawkins County Public Schools*

In *Mozert v. Hawkins County Public Schools*, a group of fundamentalist Christian parents requested that they be provided with alternative reading instruction to that being used in their local public schools. Specifically, they argued that the inclusion of certain fantasy and folk lore materials, as well as the way in which women were portrayed, violated their religious belief systems. The school board responded to the objections of the fundamentalist parents by unanimously adopting a resolution requiring all teachers to use only those instructional materials prescribed by the board. The parents and their children were denied alternative instructional materials.[62]

The fundamentalist families in *Mozert v. Hawkins County Public Schools* won their case on the basis that their religious beliefs were sincere and the school district had no compelling reason in terms of the public good to restrict them from pursuing their religious beliefs. Fundamentalists children could have been provided with reasonable alternative reading programs, or permitted to pursue a program of home reading as allowed under Tennessee law.[63]

*Mozert v. Hawkins Public Schools* was overturned by the federal appeals court in Cincinnati in August of 1986. The case clearly points to the complexity underlying censorship cases. What is ultimately at issue in these cases, and in the book banning protests in general, is whose view of culture and society shall predominate? When confounded by First Amendment rights of both groups involved—liberals and conservatives—the issue becomes almost impossible to deal with.

Is there a solution to the selection problem? Ultra-fundamentalists clearly have the right to decide what their children are taught or not taught. But do they have the right to set the curriculum standards for others in the school system? What about the rights of teachers, of authors, of publishers? Is academic freedom possible or desirable?

## CENSORSHIP VERSUS SELECTION

An important question arises as to the difference between the censorship and the selection of materials for use in the schools. The distinction between the two was made quite clear by Lester Asheim over three decades ago:

> Selection...begins with a presumption in favor of liberty of thought; censorship with a presumption in favor of thought control. Selection's approach to the book is positive, seeking its value in the book as a book and in the book as a whole. Censorship's approach is negative, seeking for vulnerable characteristics wherever they can be found—anywhere within the book, or even outside of it. Selection seeks to protect the right of the

reader to read; censorship seeks to protect—not the right—but the reader
himself from the fancied effects of his reading. The selector has faith in the
intelligence of the reader, the censor has faith only in his own.[64]

Asheim argues that selection is democratic, while censorship is authoritarian in nature. As part of the democratic tradition in America greater
faith has been placed in the selector than the censor.[65]

As mentioned earlier, censors feel that there is little or no distinction
between censorship and selection. To them what is selection for one
individual is often censorship for another. Edward Jenkinson, however,
points to significant differences between censors and selectors. Censors
search for materials they want to discard, while selectors examine
materials looking for what best meets their educational objectives. Censors
often judge works on the basis of a limited number of passages which they
find offensive. Censors rely on the reviews of other censors, while selectors
rely on reviews in professional journals. Censors believe that they know
what is right for all people, while selectors look for works that represent a
number of points of view. Censors look for reasons outside of the work to
reject it (their religion, political affiliation, etc.), while selectors judge a
work on its own merits.[66]

Conservatives such as Phyllis Schafly argue that the censorship issue
has been used by liberals to gain easy access to media:

Like the thief who cries "Stop, thief" in order to distract attention from
his own crime, many powerful liberals cry "censorship" in order to hide
the fact that *they* are the most ruthless censors of all.[67]

Schafly's comments need to be considered. The case of *Mozert v. Hawkins
County Schools* provides clear evidence of the rights of the ultra-
fundamentalists being restricted because of a school system's insistence
that all children study the same curriculum. In a democracy such as the
United States, minority groups are guaranteed their rights along with
those of the majority. If, however, ultra-fundamentalist groups expect
their rights to be maintained, then they have the obligation and duty not to
impose their value and belief systems on others.

There are few simple answers to the problem without accommoda-
tions and compromises being adopted by all of those involved. Edward
Jenkinson, for example, has pointed out that textbook censors, as any
citizens, have the right to complain about the content of textbooks, but
that their rights only extend to their own children. If an individual does not
like the content of what their children are learning, then he or she should be
able to object and ask for an alternative assignment. According to

Jenkinson, however, this does not mean that one's rights as a parent "extend to all children in the classroom, or in the school, or in the state, or in the nation."[68]

Pluralism is an essential element of our culture and society. Censors, whether liberal or conservative, want to deny this pluralism. The public school system in the United States—because of its need to serve many different people, with many different needs and beliefs—cannot effectively cope with the types of tensions and contradictions imposed on it by censors. Nor, as evidenced in the *Mozert v. Hawkins*, can it afford to act as censor itself.

We must ask ourselves, what is the ultimate goal of the ultra-fundamentalist censors. Are they really interested in the content of the curriculum of the public schools, or is the censorship issue and the banning of textbooks part of a larger issue involving their desire to more firmly establish their value and belief systems within the larger culture? Is the ultra-fundamentalist controversy over the role of public education simply part of a larger battle over the definition and meaning of American society?

# Chapter Three

# *Textbooks and the Curriculum*

---

The content of textbooks is a highly sensitive issue in any culture. They serve as one of the most traditional means by which a society preserves its values, traditions and beliefs. More often than not, they mirror what is considered acceptable or unacceptable by the society at large. Ultimately, they are a reflection of the culture for whom they are written.[1]

During the 1960s, largely as a result of the impact of the Civil Rights Movement, special interest groups lobbied successfully to eliminate racial and sexual stereotypes from textbooks. While the efforts of these groups have diminished in recent years, pressure has increased from ultra-fundamentalist organizations such as the Moral Majority, Phyllis Schafly's Eagle Forum and others who are concerned with the value and belief systems that are emphasized in the textbooks widely used in the public schools of the United States.

Ironically, the success of the liberal activists during the 1960s and 1970s in changing the content of textbooks contributed significantly to the development of an ultra-fundamentalist countermovement. It is important to remember the extraordinary social and curricular changes that have taken place in America's public schools since the early 1960s. In rural areas, small schools have often been replaced by large consolidated systems. Radical changes in traditional course content were introduced into almost every area of the school curriculum. In social studies, for example, students were encouraged through techniques such as the Inquiry Method to discuss and debate ideas rather than simply memorize historical facts and interpretations. For the first time courses in sex and drug education were introduced into the schools on a wide-scale basis.

Innovative math and science curriculums—often highly controversial—
were also introduced. For many ultra-fundamentalists even the best of the
new curriculums were seen as being antifamily, anti-God, anti-government
and immoral.[2]

Major social changes were taking place in the schools as well. Racial
integration became widespread throughout the country as the federal
government began to enforce the 1954 Supreme Court decision that
segregated schools were inherently discriminatory. The Viet Nam War
radicalized many students and teachers. American culture went through as
profound and gut-wrenching a period of social change as any since the
Civil War.

For many people a traditional and comfortable society was lost. The
new society that emerged in its place denied the superiority of the White
Race and of Men over Women. It questioned our military might and the
foundations of much of our culture's traditional wisdom and knowledge.
A backlash against these changes from the fundamentalist Christians was
perhaps inevitable.

Ultra-fundamentalist critics began to develop coherent critiques of the
public schools on a number of different levels. Of particular concern to
them was the curricular content of textbooks, a topic which has become
most closely associated among the ultra-fundamentalists with Mel and
Norma Gabler of Longview, Texas.

## THE GABLERS

Mel and Norma Gabler, more than any other ultra-fundamentalists,
have led the debate concerning what should or should not be included in
textbooks used by the public schools. Their interest in textbook reform has
occupied nearly all of their energy since the early 1960s. The Gablers
entered the field of textbook reform in the fall of 1961. At that time Mel
Gabler worked as a clerk for an oil company. Norma Gabler kept house
and raised their three sons.

Norma had graduated from high school and Mel had attended one
year of college. Both were active in "Bible-believing churches." After many
years of moving because of Mel's job, they settled in Hawkins, Texas in
1958 where Mel served as a deacon and Sunday School teacher in his
church and eventually president of the local PTA, and Norma worked as
superintendent of the youth department of the same church.[3] In the fall of
1961, Jim, the Gabler's oldest son came home complaining that something
was wrong with his history textbook *Our Nation's Story* published by the
Laidlaw Brothers publishing company. On examining the book, Mel

objected to the chapter on the Constitution which enumerated the powers granted to the federal government and the limitations placed upon the states. Nothing was included on the rights granted to the states and the limitations placed upon the federal government.[4] Mel passed the book on to Norma and she became equally upset. They found little of the traditional content in this and other textbooks that they eventually examined. Nathan Hale's statement, "I regret I have but one life to lose for my country," and Patrick Henry's "Give me liberty or give me death," were excluded. Traditional patriotic values were down-played as far as the Gablers were concerned. In their place was an emphasis on modern history, the benevolence of the federal government and the world brotherhood being created by the United Nations. The threat of World Communism was barely addressed.[5]

The Gablers began to compare their son's textbooks with history books published in 1885 and 1921. What they found was that the basic information included in these works did not agree with the more modern textbooks their son used.[6] When they protested about the content of their son's books to the local school superintendent, they were told that the books that were being used in the local school district were from an approved state list, and that if they had objections to their content they should take their objections to the State Board of Education in Austin.

Texas is one of twenty-two states in the country that use centralized methods of approving textbooks. This sytem, which involves the approval of textbooks by a review committee at the state level, dates back to the nineteenth century. Originally, its purpose was to make it possible for a state to negotiate a cheaper price for textbooks that were purchased in large quantities from a single publisher, as well as to make sure that minimal standards were adhered to in terms of textbook content.

Under the Texas system, the State Board of Education issues a textbook proclamation each spring. In the proclamation, the subjects and grade level for which new books will be selected that year are included, as well as an invitation to publishers to submit any books that they wish to have considered. A fifteen member committee, at least eight of whom are classroom teachers, evaluate the books to be considered. Citizens are invited to submit written "bills of particulars" containing specific complaints about the content of any of the textbooks that are under consideration for adoption.[7]

Norma Gabler attended hearings for the textbook committee for the first time in January of 1962. At the hearings she compared her son Jim's American history textbook *Our Nation's Story* with Barne's *A Brief History of the United States* published in 1885. According to her, the 1962 text placed a much greater emphasis on the powers of the federal government than the older book. After scrutinizing Ginn and Company's textbook *American History for High School* (1961) she complained about its emphasis on material values and its failure to discuss the Christian and spiritual values upon which the country was founded. Objecting that many of the authors of the textbooks being reviewed incorporated their political views into the content of their works, Norma questioned why it was that "almost without exception, Big Government is treated as desirable?" and why "the foundation of our nation on a heritage of Christian principles is generally slighted or ignored."[8]

As part of the 1963 textbook hearings, the Gablers questioned the content of textbooks that were being proposed for adoption that emphasized the "new math." According to them, the materials included in the new math curriculum had the potential to destroy young students' belief in the possibility of there being such a concept as an absolute. As they explained:

> On a moral basis there is fear that such abstract teaching to young minds will tend to destroy the student's belief in absolutes—to believe that nothing is concrete. This could be instrumental in helping erode their faith in other absolutes such as Christian faith.[9]

In the following year, the Gablers raised objections at the textbook hearings to the Biological Science Curriculum Study (BSCS) group textbooks that were being introduced for the first time. These books, which were part of a federally funded initiative to improve the quality of science education throughout the country, included a particular emphasis on evolutionary theory. Norma argued that equal time should be given to those who supported a Biblical or creationist interpretation of biology and those defending evolution. Why from a parent's point of view, Norma asked, should students be taught atheism in their textbooks? "Why," she asked the textbook committee, "Is it unfair to teach creation theory to a child? Why can't they teach that?"[10] Despite the protests of the Gablers and others, the BSCS biology textbooks were adopted for use in Texas.

At first the Gablers attracted relatively little attention to their complaints. They persisted, however, in their protests and by the early 1970s began to see their efforts bear fruit not only influencing which books were being adopted in Texas, but also the types of materials that were included in textbooks by publishers at a national level. Beginning in 1970, publishers of science books that included materials on evolution were required to also include an introductory statement that explained that evolution was a theory and not a fact. Publishers were also told that textbooks that contained "offensive language" would not be adopted.

Likewise in 1970 twenty regional centers were established throughout Texas where textbooks under review could be examined by the public.[11]

In 1973 the Gablers founded Educational Research Analysts, Incorporated, a nonprofit tax exempt organization. Running the organization from their house, they quickly extended their work to the national level. By the late 1970s they were supervising a staff of six, managing a mailing list of 10,000 names and receiving an average of twenty to fifty pieces of mail each day.[12]

The Gabler's philosophy of education is relatively straight forward. They maintain that the purpose of education is "the imparting of factual knowledge, basic skills and cultural heritage."[13] In documents such as their 1983 publication "Humanism in Textbooks: Secular Religion in the Classroom" one can see their ideas concerning textbooks and their content summarized quite clearly. In this work, they maintain that "Humanists enthusiastically seek to remake the world in man's image."[14] Drawing on quotes from textbooks put out by a wide-range of publishers, and also a wide-range of grade levels and subject areas, they argued that there is a conscious effort in the works cited to indoctrinate students in specifically humanist values.

Under the category of "Evolution" they object to a 1977 high school psychology textbook that explained that:

> Infants can grasp an object such as a finger, so strongly, that they can be lifted in to the air. We suspect that this reflex is left over from an earlier stage in human evolution, when babies had to cling to their ape-like mothers' coat while mothers were climbing or searching for food."[15]

Similarly, a 1978 Harper and Row high school textbook *Psychology Today and Tomorrow* was criticized for stating that "From an evolutionary viewpoint, smell is one of the most primitive of the senses."[16]

In protesting the content of these textbooks, the Gablers specifically made reference to Scripture as a source of authority. According to them, quotes such as those cited above violate the Biblical principle that God created man in his own image (Gen 1:1 and Gen 1:27, Jer 1:4-5). In reference to "Self Authority (Individual Autonomy)" the Gabler's objected to the notion that they feel that many textbooks promote "the belief that man is his own authority and is not accountable to any higher power."[17] Citing a 1969 eighth grade basal reader published by Ginn, they objected to the following activity as a reflection of an emphasis on self authority:

> Think of a situation that would probably result in a difference between yourself and your parents. How would you defend your position? With

what arguments would your parents counter? Write a dialogue between
your parents and yourself.[18]

Under the category of "Sexual Permissiveness," the Gabler's objected
to the fact that according to Humanist values "all forms of sexual
expression are acceptable."[19] Specific objections were raised by them to
statements such as the comment in *Life and Health*, a 1976 textbook for
ninth and tenth graders published by Random House that "Divorce is
considered an acceptable way of solving a problem."[20] In the same
textbook they also criticized the statement: "A person with variant sexual
interests is not necessarily bad, sick, or mentally ill."[21] In this case, they cite
James 1:15 to the effect that: "when lust hath conceived, it bringeth forth
sin; and sin, when it is finished, bringeth forth death."[22]

Other topics raised by the Gablers in "Humanism in Textbooks"
include "Situation Ethics," "Distorted Realism," "Anti-Biblical Bias,"
"Anti-Free Enterprise," "One-World Government," and "Death Education." In large part, the protests of the Gablers are focused on the definition
of what values are to be taught to the children in our schools. No
consideration is given on their part to the diversity and pluralism inherent
in American society. Their assumption as ultra-fundamentalists is that
Christianity and the value system it promotes is the sole source of values
that should be promoted in American society. In protesting the right to
establish their own point of view, they tend to disregard the values and
belief systems of others. Alternate religious beliefs to Christianity are
evidently unacceptable to them, as are the possibilities of an agnostic or
atheistic view of the world.

According to William Martin, the Gabler's attack on moral and
cultural relativism is aimed primarily at the social sciences.[23] In large part,
they are attempting to hold on to a simpler model of American society—
one that probably has never existed in this country in which there is a
consensus in terms of moral values and religious beliefs. Undoubtedly
many of their concerns are an outgrowth of the crisis of values and beliefs
that have affected our public and private institutions since the early 1960s.
Referring to the problems of the schools, for example, Mel Gabler
maintains that:

40 years ago the problem then, as far as the student was concerned, were
such things as not putting waste paper in the wastepaper basket, or
getting out of turn in line or speaking in class. Now what do you have in
the classrooms? You have a great amount of violence and abuse and drug
problems and so forth, and something has caused that change, and we feel

its because the textbooks have totally abandoned, or almost totally abandoned, the basic traditional American values on which our nation was founded.[24]

For the Gablers, most textbooks in use in the schools are far too relativistic in the values which they promote. In "A Parent's Guide to Textbook Review and Reform," they maintain that:

> School texts currently in use by and large, tend to promote the concept that all values are relative. Steeped in this relativism, students soon are unable to distinguish between right and wrong. If, as we believe, children become what they are taught, the assault of relativistic thought on our nation's children bodes ill for the future.[25]

Arguing that many textbooks reflect an ideological perspective that maintains that the purpose of education is the promotion of social change, the Gablers argue that instead the schools should be concerned with imparting factual knowledge, basic skills and cultural heritage. Specifically, they argue against an ideology that includes, but is not limited to the following:

— analysis of the personal and familial problems of the child
— presenting life as a problem in sociology to be solved by government bureaucrats and social science experts
— treating all moral questions as open, relative and debatable
— portraying total equality as an absolute value
— consistently one-sided presentations on current political controversies
— the inevitability of change and the cliché that all change is good
— the inevitability of individual and community dependence on government in all aspects of life
— environmental determinism
— society's collective guilt for human problems
— evolution taught as fact
— stories of violence, cruelty and morbidity presented as accurate portrayals of "real life"
— attacks on Christians and church-goers as authoritarian, cruel and intolerant
— suggested classroom techniques employing humanistic techniques that violate religious freedom, e.g. role playing, diaries, death education exercises, questionnaires and values clarification games[26]

According to the Gablers, the inclusion of the above values is often accompanied by the exclusion of countervailing values such as:

— loyalty, faith, sacrifice and unselfishness
— self-reliance and pride of accomplishments
— freedom and liberty
— attachments to home and country
— limited powers of government
— religious and cultural traditions
— individual responsibility
— scientific evidence for creation[27]

In summary, the Gablers attack on the content of textbooks is ultimately rooted in their acceptance of an authoritarian approach to knowledge based on tradition and Scripture, a rejection of critical inquiry, scientific methods and relativistic models of knowledge.

Their impact has been undeniable. Through their efforts, they have accomplished more than perhaps any other set of activitists reviewing curriculum materials in the United States and have had a greater influence in shaping the content of what is published in elementary and secondary textbooks. While they consistently deny that they are censors, and maintain that "Only people in power can be censors,"[28] their impact on education in not only Texas, but the country in general has been remarkable. A case in point: their efforts to block dictionaries being approved for purchase for the public schools by the Texas Board of Education in 1976.

According to the Gablers, five dictionaries including the *American Heritage Dictionary, The Doubleday Dictionary, Webster's Seventh New Collegiate Dictionary, The Random House College Dictionary,* and *Webster's New World Dictionary of the English Language* were, in their opinion, objectionable because they included vulgar language. Mel noted, for example, that one of the definitions included for *bed* was "a place to have intercourse."[29] How a reference book, which must by definition reflect the realities of a culture and its language can avoid colloquial language and slange that is deemed inappropriate or vulgar and still fulfill its requirements as a reference text is an issue that the Gablers fail to address. In fact, it is this failure to recognize the existence of other points of view—other baselines of cultural reference and perspective that consistently characterizes the ultra-fundamentalist critique of public education.

The Gablers have consistently received the support of leading ultra-fundamentalists such as the Reverend Jerry Falwell, and the Reverend Tim LaHaye. Both have used the Gabler's research in promoting their causes.[30] Each represents a significant force within the ultra-fundamentalist movement. Each has their own separate constituency, even though their constituencies may overlap. In general, their opposition to the content of textbooks focuses on similar concerns: family versus state control over what is taught to children, the influence of secular humanism, sex education, etc. In his article "Textbooks in Public Schools: A Disgrace and Concern for America" Falwell summarized his concerns about textbooks in the following way:

> To bring charges against textbooks may sound extreme, but we should be concerned. The vast majority of Americans are the "Moral Majority.' They want America to remain a great democratic society built on (1) laws, (2) the Constitution, and (3) a devotion to truth.[31]

Falwell does not see his efforts as being those of a censor. According to him:

> To oppose textbooks is not the same as book burning. This is not an attempt to censor the books of our schools. But where there are mistakes, they must be corrected...[32]

The failure to accept the possibility of other viewpoints, in reference to the content of materials included in textbooks, is particularly evident in the work of Tim LaHaye. LaHaye is a strong supporter of the efforts of Mel and Norma Gabler. According to him, they "have probably done more to halt the spread of humanism in our school textbooks than anyone else in America."[33] It is important to note that almost everything that LaHaye writes about textbooks and their content is based on the research of the Gablers. In his work *The Battle for the Public Schools*, LaHaye lists "nine basic tenets of humanism found in our children's textbooks"—all based on research conducted by the Gablers. These include:

1. evolutionary dogma (the idea that evolution is unquestioned fact),
2. self-autonomy (the idea that children are their own authorities),
3. situation ethics (the idea that there are no moral absolutes),
4. Christianity negated (the idea that there is no supernatural),
5. sexual freedom (the idea that public sex education is necessary, but without morals, etc.),
6. total reading freedom (the idea that children should have the right to read anything),
7. death education (the idea that there is no hope after death),

8. internationalism (the idea that world citizenship is preferable to national patriotism),
9. socialism (the idea that socialism is superior to private ownership).[34]

LaHaye, uses the above material as a launching point for his own work. In fact, the basic outline for his book *The Battle for the Public Schools* conforms very closely to this list of issues developed by the Gablers. These topics are in fact perceived by many ultra-fundamentalists as being part of a larger humanistic curriculum that they believe has come to dominate American education in recent years.

## HUMANISTIC CURRICULUMS OPPOSED BY THE ULTRA-FUNDAMENTALISTS

Ultra-fundamentalist critics of the schools consistently trace the problems of contemporary school curriculums back to the work of John Dewey and the Progressive Education Movement. According to Onaleee McGraw, for example, humanistic education is simply "the latest manifestation of the so-called progressive life-adjustment philosophy" that has dominated public education for decades.[35] Supposed advocates of "humanistic education" include not only John Dewey, but Jean Piaget, Carl Rogers, Lawrence Kohlberg, Abraham Maslow, William Glaser and Jerome Bruner. For each, socialization of the child is supposedly the main purpose of education.[36] A clearer understanding of the ultra-fundamentalists' objections to Humanistic education can be gained by a careful examination of their criticisms of Values Clarification as a curriculum.

### *Values Clarification*

Values Clarification was first introduced into the schools during the 1960s. While associated with a number of educational theorists, Values Clarification can in large part trace its origins back to the work of Louis E. Raths, Merrill Harmin and Sidney B. Simon. In their book *Values and Teaching* they defined "value" as involving a seven-step sequence, a process of choosing, prizing and acting. According to them:

> in order for something to be of a value, according to the Clarifiers, a person must freely choose it from alternatives, and only after carefully considering the consequences of each alternative. In addition, the person must be happy with his values: "values flow from choices we are glad to make."[37]

Implicit in such a theory is the assumption that all moral values are relative.

In his book *The Battle for the Public Schools: Humanism's Threat to Our Children* Tim LeHaye maintains that Values Clarification:

> is really mortal man's vicious assault on the minds of our children. It is a subtle technique that combines group therapy, sensitivity training, and peer-pressure brainwashing. It attacks the moral commitment of any student, particularly the vulnerable children in our government controlled school system.[38]

Onalee McGraw objects to Values Clarification on the basis that "nothing concerning the content of values is relevant to defining what a value is."[39] According to McGraw, under the relativistic system of Values Classification one can support racism, fascism or whatever "ism" one wants to as long as one follows the appropriate procedures for the analysis of an issue. Process becomes more important than product. Absolutes are deemphasized. "There is no means within the process to find any of these value systems objectionable."[40]

Ultra-fundamentalist writers such as McGraw directly link Values Clarification to the earlier educational theorists Dewey and Piaget, and more recently to Lawrence Kohlberg. According to McGraw, it is Kohlberg's work that has "become the focus for educators committed to the pragmatism of values clarification."[41]

## Criticisms of Lawrence Kohlberg's Theory of Moral Development

According to Kohlberg, the essence of what is moral is a result of individuals moving through various stages of moral development. Drawing on research conducted over a twenty year period, Kohlberg based his theory of moral development on the results of experiments dealing with fifty people solving various moral dilemmas. According to Kohlberg there are six stages of moral development. These include:

*Preconventional Level*

STAGE 1   Punishment and obedience orientation (physical consequences determine what is good or bad).

STAGE 2   Instrumental relativist orientation (what satisfies one's own needs is good).

*Conventional Level*

STAGE 3   Interpersonal concordance or "good boy-nice girl orientation (what pleases or helps others is good).

STAGE 4   "Law and order" orientation (maintaining the social order, doing one's duty is good).

*Postconventional Level*
STAGE 5   Social contract-legalistic orientation (values agreed upon by society, including individual rights and rules for consensus, determine what is right).
STAGE 6   Universal ethical-principle orientation. Right is defined by the decision of conscience in accord with self-chosen ethical principles, appealing to logical comprehensiveness, universality and consistency.[42]

In Stage six these principles are abstracted like the Golden Rule, or the categorical imperative, rather than concretized, as is the case of the Ten Commandments.

It is Stage six that ultra-fundamentalists such as McGraw have the greatest difficulty dealing with. Citing an example from the publication *Hypothetical Dilemmas for Use in Moral Education*, prepared by colleagues of Kohlberg's at Harvard's Education and Research Center, McGraw objects to an exercise in which students are faced with a problem in situational ethics. The Johnson family (with four children) is both happy and quite close with one another. Mr. and Mrs. Johnson are in their thirties. An accident occurs in which Mr. Johnson falls from a building and is paralyzed. He is no longer able to have sexual intercourse with his wife because of the accident. The question is raised: What should Mrs. Johnson do if she does not want to give up her sex life? Options presented include getting a divorce, having an affair secretly, having an affair with her husband's knowledge, and so on. According to McGraw:

> The subjective approach to value is totally revealed in this moral dilemma; Mrs. Johnson's choice "if she does not want to give up her sex life" is to get a divorce or have extramarital affairs.[43]

Citing the work of Bennett and Delattre, McGraw criticizes the exercise as focusing entirely on Mrs. Johnson's rights and desires, while ignoring the rights and desires of her husband and her children.

McGraw objects to the work of Kohlberg and others associated with Humanistic education and, more specifically values clarification, on the basis that such work interferes with the rights of parents to raise their children according to their personal values and beliefs:

> To those for whom a created order does not exist, man determines
> through self-chosen principles, the modes of social control under which

children will be socialized in state schools. It is entirely possible for, given the propensity of the education establishment to go from one educational fad to another, that a single child in his school life could be subjected to the behavioral psychology techniques of B.F. Skinner, the humanistic "self-development" techniques of Abraham Maslow, and the insistence that he pass through the stages of moral development which have been self-chosen by Kohlberg.[44]

McGraw asks what right do educational theorists such as Kohlberg, Simon, Rogers and Bruner have "to enter the minds of other people's children?"[45]

In response to a reporter for the Los Angeles *Times* who argued that she had gone through Values Clarification training and had not been harmed by it, Tim LeHaye maintained that while as an adult her values were firmly established and in place, such would not be the case with an elementary or secondary school student whose moral values are not clearly defined and who is highly susceptible to peer pressure.[46]

Values Clarification is seen by the ultra-fundamentalists as a clear attempt to indoctrinate students with secular humanist values and beliefs. Dr. O.M. Wellman in the March 1981 edition of *Educational Research Analysts Handbook No. 2* (a copyrighted publication of "The Mel Gablers") concludes that Values Clarification:

1.  is an invasion of privacy
2.  promotes situation ethics
3.  associates concepts with greed and hypocrisy
4.  suggests and promotes immoral concepts (for example, abortion, homosexuality, and promiscuous sex are viewed as valid moral alternatives because they are presented in a positive fashion)[47]

Values clarification is seen by the ultra-fundamentalists as a means by which secular humanists are attempting to act as "change agents in the schools." They feel that this problem is particularly evident in the social studies curriculum developed by the psychologist Jerome Bruner and colleagues called "Man a Course of Study" (MACOS).

### *"Man," A Course of Study*

In 1963 a number of scholars were brought together by Jerome Bruner to discuss the possibility of developing a new humanities and social science curriculum that could be used by the schools throughout the country. That meeting produced an exploratory proposal which was presented to the National Science Foundation. Eventually the NSF, a federal agency, awarded a grant of $4.8 million to develop a new curriculum for fifth and sixth graders.

MACOS was designed as a full year program intended to help fifth and sixth graders explore fundamental questions about human behavior. In addition to traditional printed material, it used films, tapes, games and dramatic devices. The curriculum focused on the study of the Netsilik Eskimos, a group of Native Americans from the Pelly Bay region in Canada. Through a careful examination of the culture of the Netsiliks, it was hoped that students would be able to explore basic questions about the nature of human beings, their life styles, patterns of social interaction, child rearing and cosmology.[48]

The MACOS curriculum was deliberately open-ended and intended to have students act as problem solvers. They were asked to compare and contrast what it was that they learned in the various parts of the curriculum, to develop their own interpretations and to examine their own values and beliefs in reference to the materials they were studying. Much of the material included in the curriculum was controversial. The course materials examined religious issues, as well as questions related to reproduction, aggression and murder.[49]

The Netsilik culture is profoundly different from traditional Western society. Much of their social behavior is an adaption to the extraordinarily harsh environment in which they live. Senilicide and infanticide are practiced—seemingly of necessity if the group is to survive. According to Bruner, the purpose of the curriculum was:

> to lead the children to understand how man goes about understanding his world, making sense of it; that one kind of explanation is no more human than another.[50]

According to Bruner and his colleagues, the rules by which men and women live vary according to the different conditions which they must face.[51]

As a curriculum MACOS tends to refute the notion of absolute values. In addition, it bases many of its interpretations on the assumption that evolution is a useful theory that can explain a great deal in not only the natural sciences, but the social sciences as well. MACOS, because of its controversial content, could not get the sponsorship of commercial publishers, who were evidently concerned about the response by the general public to its controversial content. Funding for its publication was finally obtained through the National Science Foundation, and the materials were put out by Bruner and his colleagues.[52]

Between 1970 and 1974, approximately 1,700 schools in forty-seven states were using the MACOS curriculum. By 1975, however, protests were flaring up all over the country concerning the use of the curriculum in the schools.[53] Dorothy Nelkin in her book *The Creation Controversy: Science or Scripture in the Schools* has outlined in detail the protests that developed over the use of the MACOS curriculum in towns such as Corinth, New York and Lake City, Florida. Specifically, these and similar protests elsewhere in the country objected to the fact that it:

1. taught that man is an animal,
2. taught disturbing values (i.e. that power and violence are necessary for survival),
3. undermined parental authority, and
4. substituted radical educational ideas in the place of traditional values.[54]

Although protests over the MACOS curriculum occured at the local level, the Gablers also promptly criticized it.[55] According to Norma Gabler:

> If this depraved course, filled with violence and death, is "one of the best series to be developed for use in our schools," parents had better become concerned about our nation's future, which is our children.[56]

Specifically, Gabler objected to the inclusion in the curriculum of information related to wife-swapping, adultery, cannibalism and euthanasia.[57] Tim LaHaye, cites a fifth grade teacher Sheila Burgers, who had used the curriculum in her classes in Sheffield, Massachusetts, to the effect that:

> Defenders of MACOS insist that the teaching materials give children an opportunity to compare different life styles, to become tolerant of moral values. The defenders never mention 10-year olds have not studied Western civilization, and have no formal training in the history, technology, or social structure of their world.[58]

LaHaye argues that:

> Any nonhumanist can see the Netsiliks are almost extinct because of their life-style. One cannot violate traditional moral values indefinitely without bearing the consequences. But that fact is not permitted in this values-clarification specialty.[59]

Implicit in LaHaye's comment is the assumption that "traditional moral values," i.e. Christian ultra-fundamentalist values, must be followed in all cases, or one must suffer the consequences.

Pedagogically, the MACOS curriculum is highly controversial in nature. Whether one is an ultra-fundamentalist, an agnostic or an atheist, it represents a significant departure from more traditional instructional materials. It is clear in the case of the ultra-fundamentalists, that their objections to the curriculum stem from their belief that its content and meaning represents an infringement on their personal belief systems. For many ultra-fundamentalists the MACOS curriculum represents a demonstrable example of secular humanists attempting to work as agents of social change in the schools.

The belief on the part of the ultra-fundamentalists that the public school system is deliberately trying to reshape the values of students through the content of curriculum is repeated over and over again in their publications. Besides Values Clarification and the MACOS curriculum, topics such as Global Education, Death Education, Evolution and Sex Education are frequently cited as areas of concern. The ultra-fundamentalist response to Evolution is discussed in subsequent chapters of this book. Before completing this chapter, however, a brief analysis of the ultra-fundamentalist's reaction to Death Education is necessary.

*Death Education*

Teaching children about death as a subject in the public schools is a topic that is seen by many ultra-fundamentalists as a continuation of the assault on basic Christian values associated with Values Clarification. Authors such as Tim LaHaye ask what relevance the subject has to traditional education? According to him, Death Education's real purpose is to eliminate the "natural fear of death and Judgement Day."[60] LaHaye asks fundamentalist parents whether or not they want "a humanist teacher, one who rejects all absolutes"[61] and who may be hostile toward a belief in God, the Bible and Jesus Christ asking their children about questions related to life after death, their belief in heaven or hell, whether they think about death and whether or not they have ever contemplated suicide.[62] According to LaHaye:

> These and other questions are cleverly utilized by humanistic missionaries (masquerading as schoolteachers) on our captive children in the seventh to the twelfth grades; the questions serve as springboards to teaching their anti-Christian concepts in our public schools. They are nothing more than a devious means to indoctrinate our youth with their anti-God religion.[63]

LaHaye goes on to argue that he doesn't pay property and income taxes to subsidize "heretical teachings of the religion of humanism."[64]

According to the Gablers, discussions of death as included in many public school textbooks frequently violate the Biblical principle "that there shall be a resurrection of the dead, both of the just and unjust." (Act 24:15) and that all those who hate the Lord love death. (Proverbs 8:36)[65] Citing a 1976 ninth and tenth grade Random House textbook entitled *Life and Health*, they object to discussions that suggest that the thought of death sometimes occurs in a sexual context, and that orgasm like dying, "involves a surrender to the involuntary and the unknown."[66] In a 1980 edition of the same book, they object to the fact that in death "the individual experiences a cosmic consciousness, characterized by a sense of unity with other people, nature, and the universe; a feeling of being outside time and space; and the extraordinary feelings of contentment and ecstasy."[67]

Citing the MACOS curriculum, the Gablers specifically object to discussions of euthanasia and senilicide among the Netsilik eskimos, as well as discussions of cannibalism.[68] According to them, death education is unacceptable because it supports "the belief that there is no hope of existence beyond the grave—no heaven or hell; endorses euthanasia and suicide."[69] Critics such as Barbara Morris ask: "How can a subject so value-laden be treated adequately or fairly in government schools that are committed to a one-sided Humanist view of life?"[70]

For Morris, death education is seen as having the potential to encourage students to not only accept the concepts of euthanasia but also abortion.[71] Tim LaHaye maintains that the reason the "humanists" teach death education is that:

1.  it is an excellent way to attack traditional beliefs in God and salvation,
2.  it provides an excellent means of preparing young people to act like nihilistic hedonists,
3.  it provides individuals an excellent introduction into the possibilities of suicide, and
4.  it encourages the acceptance of euthanasia.[72]

In reading authors such as the Gablers, LaHaye and Morris, one finds oneself asking the question of what it is that they think the humanists have as their purpose in promoting death education? For LaHaye, the acceptance of euthanasia represents the first step in a larger process of eliminating undesirables from the society:

Once euthanasia has become an accepted norm, the next step will be to rid society of the "undesirables." This would include the helpless, mental

incompetents, and those who oppose "progress"—like Christians and
other traditional moral activists who do not approve of homosexuality
and radical feminism or do not agree with antimoral humanists.[73]

Citing the work of Francis Schaeffer, LaHaye maintains that the parallels
between the genocide committed by the Facists in Germany during the
1930s and 1940s is no different than what contemporary humanists are
proposing:

> Germans did not murder their elderly, the impaired, infants, and their
> undesirable countrymen because they were Germans, but because they
> were *humanists*. Some American humanists are fully capable of the same
> actions. Already over 10 million unborn children have been murdered in
> the name of abortion, thanks to humanistic thinkers on the Supreme
> Court. We are less than two decades away from infanticide and
> euthanasia, if we allow humanists to remain in control of our country.[74]

The ultra-fundamentalist concern over the content of textbooks, and the
curriculum in general, is in fact part of their larger concern about the threat
posed by secular humanism to American culture and society. What is at
work is a genuine belief on their part that an overwhelming conspiracy is at
work to subvert traditional Christian values and culture and to create a
Godless and sin-ridden nation. Leaders of this movement are humanist
educators, media figures and political leaders who are acting as agents of
deliberate and systematic social change.

## CHANGE AGENTS IN THE SCHOOLS

Tim LaHaye in his book *The Battle for the Public Schools* cites a
"Carter administration educrat" to the effect that:

> One of the reasons that we need to establish pre-school day-care centers
> for children from three years up is because in spite of billions of dollars at
> our disposal and the thirteen years we have the children in public schools,
> we are still unable to undo the harm done to them before they arrive in
> kindergarten.[75]

LaHaye maintains that the harm done to children involves "a belief in
God, an absolute value system, patriotism, and respect for the authority of
parenthood."[76] For LaHaye this process represents a clear demonstration
of the attempt of secular humanists to act as change agents within the
schools. Curriculums such as Values Clarification and Death Education, as

well as more specific materials such as MACOS become the main means by which students are indoctrinated.

Among the ultra-fundamentalist theorists, the role of schools as Change Agents has been most clearly outlined by Barbara M. Morris. In her book *Change Agents in the Schools,* Morris describes a change agent as "a person, organization, or institution that changes or helps to change the beliefs, values, attitudes or behavior of people without their knowledge or consent."[77] According to Morris, the purpose of most of the activity of not only public, but also private schools, is to eliminate existing belief systems and replace them with new values and beliefs that will "render the child susceptible to manipulation, coercion, control and corruption for the rest of his life.[78]

Morris's theory of the schools as Change Agents maintains that in reality the public schools are not controlled by the people in a community, but that instead they are administrative agencies of the state and/or federal government. Public schools, according to Morris, are in fact governmental schools, and governmental schools:

> are administrative governmental agencies that exist to promote change. What kinds of change? Social change, political change, economic change, cultural change, religious change, change in our form of government. *Total change.*[79]

Specifically, government schools are seen as instruments that have as their primary purpose the destruction of the status, structure and stability of the family. By weakening the family, it is possible for "the proposed dictatorship to be established and maintained."[80]

We cannot understand the ultra-fundamentalist critique of textbooks and the content of the curriculum unless we ultimately consider their position in the context of their belief that American culture and society is being subverted by a conspiracy of secular humanists. For many of the ultra-fundamentalists a holy war is being waged—one for which there can be no compromise or retreat. The public schools are the battleground on which the holy war is being fought. Textbooks and the curriculum are the tools of social change that must be opposed at all costs. Guidance can come only through the Holy Spirit. As Henry Morris argues:

> Since we ourselves are sinners, our students and their parents are sinners, and the researchers and the textbook writers also are sinners, how are we now to discern the truth in order to teach it?...The answer is by the Holy Spirit, through the Scriptures inspired by Him.[81]

If God is denied entry to the public school, then it follows that there can be no Truth in what is taught in those schools, and that ultimately secular humanist instruction represents the denial of Christianity and ultimately of salvation.

Clearly, the ultra-fundamentalists' concern about the content of textbooks and other curricular materials reflects what is perceived by them as an extraordinarily serious issue, one that not only involves the very definition of American culture, but even the salvation of their children and their children's children. Many of them believe that the content of school textbooks and curriculum represent "a complete usurpation of parental rights and negation of constitutional guarantees."[82]

A number of difficult questions are raised by the ultra-fundamentalists' position. To what extent do parents have the right to be involved in the process of selecting what is or is not taught to their children in the public schools? Related to this question is the issue of whose values should predominate in the public schools? What are the rights of minority and majority groups in the selection of textbooks and other related school materials? What are the implications of censorship by any group? Should highly vocal and manipulative critics like the Gablers be allowed to exert the type of influence that they do? Where does selection begin and censorship end? An attempt to look at these questions in greater detail is the subject of the subsequent chapters in this book.

# Chapter Four

# *Creationism and the Schools*

Among the most controversial issues involving the ultra-fundamentalists in the past decade has been their effort to introduce Creationism into the curriculum of the public schools. Although the teaching of Creationism may appear to be a new issue, it is in fact part of a larger debate involving religion and evolutionary theory that dates back to the middle of the nineteenth century.

The debate began with Charles Darwin and his publication in 1859 of *The Origins of the Species.* Until the advent of Darwin, science was primarily rooted in theology. Its purpose was to demonstrate the existence of God. It did so, according to advocates of a literal or Biblical interpretation of Creation, by demonstrating evidence of God's design and influence in nature.[1] Darwin's work represented a radical challenge to this traditional theistic interpretation of science.

The debate concerning evolution versus creationism centers on two very different understandings of the origin of life and the nature of the universe. Although seldom stated in these terms, it is ultimately a debate over ways of knowing the world.[2] The distinction between each of these systems is made quite clear by the Creationist Henry Morris:

> Evolutionism is the philosophy that purports to explain the origins and development of all things in terms of continuing natural processes in a self-existing universe. Creationism, on the other hand, explains the origin and development of all things by completed supernatural processes in a universe created and sustained by a transcendent, self-existing Creator.[3]

While the debate over evolutionary versus biblical models of creation remained a serious issue in both Europe and America throughout the nineteenth century, it was the defeat of anti-evolutionary forces in the "Scopes Monkey Trial" in 1923 that led proevolutionary groups to assume that the Biblical or Creationist model (that had largely prevailed up until that time) was no longer widely accepted. Significantly, the issues debated in the Scopes trial differ little from those that are evident in the current controversy over secular humanism and public education. At the Scopes trial, for example, William Jennings Bryan defended a Creationist point of view by asking:

> What right, have the evolutionists—a relatively small percentage of the population—to teach at public expense a so called scientific interpretation of the Bible, when orthodox Christians are not permitted to teach an orthodox interpretation of the Bible.[4]

Although the Scopes trial is widely perceived as a victory for those advocating a more "modernist" interpretation of science, the teaching of evolution in the public schools actually declined after 1925. A 1942 national survey of high school biology teachers indicated that less than 50 percent of high school biology teachers in the United States were teaching about organic evolution in their courses. As late as 1959, one hundred years after the publication of *The Origins of the Species*, Herman J. Muller wrote that public school biology teaching remained dominated by "antiquated religious traditions."[5] In fact, until the late 1960s, in both Arkansas and Mississippi, laws were enforced making the teaching of evolution illegal. This situation was challenged in 1966 in the case of *Epperson v. State of Arkansas*.


## EPPERSON VERSUS STATE OF ARKANSAS

In *Epperson v. State of Arkansas*, a first year high school biology teacher, Susan Epperson, challenged the 1928 law prohibiting the teaching of evolution arguing that it was unconstitutional and violated the federal guarantee of free speech. Epperson received support from the Little Rock Ministerial Association, which stated that: "to use the Bible to support an irrational and archaic concept of static and undynamic creation is not only to misunderstand the meaning of the Book of Genesis, but to do God and religion a disservice by making both the enemies of scientific advancement and academic freedom."[6] Epperson won her case in the Chancery Court of Pulaski County. This decision was overturned, however, by the State

Supreme Court. Epperson appealed the case to the Federal Supreme Court.

Epperson testified that she brought the law suit before the Court: "because I have a Text Book which includes the theory about the origin of the descent or the ascent of man from the lower animals. This seemed to be a widely accepted theory and I felt it my responsibility to acquaint students with it."[7] Justice Fortas delivered the Court's verdict, which maintained that the courts should not intervene in conflicts resulting from the daily running of the public schools unless they involved basic constitutional values. According to Fortas:

> Judicial interposition in the operation of the public school system of the Nation raises problems requiring care and restraint. Our courts, however, have not failed to apply the First Amendment's mandate in our educational system where essential to safeguard the fundamental values of freedom of speech and inquiry and of belief. By and large, public education in our Nation is committed to the control of state and local authorities. Courts do not and cannot intervene in the resolution of conflicts which arise in the daily operation of school systems and which do not directly and sharply implicate basic constitutional values.[8]

Fortas noted, however, that despite this fact the First Amendment "does not tolerate laws that cast a pall of orthodoxy over the classroom."[9]

Fortas argued that Arkansas sought to prevent teachers from discussing the theory of evolution because it was contrary to the belief of certain individuals that the Book of Genesis was the soul source of understanding concerning the origin of man. According to Fortas:

> No suggestion has been made that Arkansas' law may be justified by considerations of state policy other than the religious views of some of its citizens. It is clear that fundamentalist sectarian conviction was and is the law's reason for existence.[10]

The basic constitutional issue involved in the case was freedom of speech. According to Fortas, under the Arkansas anti-evolution statute, the knowledge made available to children in the schools would be circumscribed and limited.[11]

The *Epperson* decision was seen in the national media as an issue that should have been buried with the Scopes trial. *Time* magazine suggested that the case "seemed to come from another era," while *Newsweek* reported that "finally last week, forty-three years after Scopes's conviction, the Supreme Court struck down one of the monkey laws."[12] Attempts were made to maintain anti-evolutionary statutes in Mississippi, but based on the precedent of *Epperson* the Mississippi Supreme Court ruled on December 21, 1970 that:

> we are constrained to follow the decisions of the Supreme Court of the United States....It is clear to us from what was said in *Epperson* that the Supreme Court of the United States has for all practical purposes already held that our antievolution statutes are unconstitutional.[13]

Seemingly, the antievolutionary forces had suffered a major defeat. In fact, the battle simply was entering a new phase.

## CREATION SCIENCE AS AN ALTERNATIVE TO BIBLICAL CREATIONISM

The significance of *Epperson v. Arkansas* was that it guaranteed that evolution would have a place in the science curriculums of the nation's schools. The Creationists countered with a totally new tactic, arguing that Creationism was capable of being confirmed through scientific studies. California was the arena in which this new battle was fought.

During the middle and late 1960s, the California State Board of Education was under the conservative leadership of its Superintendent of Public Instruction, Max Rafferty. In a booklet prepared under his direction in 1969 entitled *Guidelines for Moral Instruction in California Schools*, Rafferty asserted his belief that American culture was built on the Bible and its teachings.[14] According to the booklet, progressive education, sex education, evolutionary teachings and related curriculums were undermining the basic morality and values system outlined by the Founding Fathers.[15]

At the same time that Rafferty's *Guidelines for Moral Instruction* were being prepared, the California State Advisory Committee on Science Education was at work on a different document that was eventually published as the *Science Framework for California Public Schools Kindergarten—Grades One Through Twelve*.[16] Among the distinguished scientists and educators that contributed to this document were Wallace R. Brode (American Chemical Society), Jacob Bronowski (Salk Institute), Robert M. Gagne (University of California, Berkeley), Ralph W. Gerard (University of California, Irvine), Paul DeHart Hurd (Stanford), Ray D. Owen (California Institute of Technology) and Henry Rapoport (University of California, Berkeley).[17]

When the *Science Framework* was presented to the State Board of Education in the fall of 1969, it gave the creationists an opportunity to make sure that creation theory concepts were incorporated into science curriculums in the state. Several of the members of the Board urged that the *Science Framework* not be accepted unless "creation Science" was given a place in the document. Objections to the document were raised by Vernon Grose who argued that specific sections supported evolutionary theory. Grose's objections were received sympathetically by the State Board of Education. Key sections dealing with evolution were eliminated from the *Science Framework* draft and new sections on creation and evolution developed by Grose were substituted in their place. Grose's substitute material maintained that the origin of life implies a dualism "or the necessity to use several theories" to explain it:

> While the Bible and other philosophic treatises also mention creation, science has independently postulated the various theories of creation. Therefore creation in scientific terms is not a religious or philosophic belief. Also note that creation and evolutionary theories are not necessarily mutually exclusive. Some of the scientific data (e.g., the regular absence of transitional forms) may be best explained by a creation theory, while other data (e.g. transmutation of species) substantiate a process of evolution.[18]

This and other additions made by Grose to the *Science Framework* gave California creationists the means by which to demand that their views on science be included in the public school curriculum.

The creationists eventually began to call the body of "scientific" information supporting biblical creation either "scientific creationism" or "creation science." Recognizing the need to develop new curriculum materials for the schools, Nell and Kelly Segraves joined together in 1970 with Henry Morris to form the Creation Science Research Center. Nell Segraves had achieved notoriety seven years earlier in 1963 when, together with another California woman Jean Sumrall, she attempted to challenge the restrictions placed on school prayer by the recent Supreme Court decision of *Abington School District v. Schempp*. For a number of years before the issuing of the *Science Framework* draft Morris had served as president of the Creation Research Society.[19]

The Creation-Science Research Center was set up as an arm of the newly created Christian Heritage College which had been established just outside San Diego in El Cajon by Tim LaHaye. Since the early 1970s it has served as a center for research and the dissemination of creation science materials.[20] Philosophical differences between Segraves and Morris eventually led to Christian Heritage College establishing the Institute for Creation Research—an organization totally separate from the Creation-

Science Research Center. Today the two organizations, one under the leadership of Segraves and the other under the leadership of Morris function completely independently of one another.[21]

According to Morris, evolution has no basis in scientific fact—instead it is a false philosophy which ultimately distorts the framework of contemporary public education and schooling. As he explains:

> One of the most amazing phenomenon in the history of education is that a speculative philosophy based on no true scientific evidence could have been universally adopted and taught as a scientific fact, in all the public schools. This philosophy has been made the very framework of modern education and the underlying premise in all textbooks. It contitutes the present world-view of liberal intellectuals in every field.[22]

Since neither Evolution nor Creationism can ultimately be proven, or tested scientifically, Morris believes that both must be accepted on faith and as a result, are religious in nature.[23] As he explains:

> Neither evolution nor creation is accessible to the scientific method, since they deal with origins and history, not with presently observable and repeatable events.[24]

For Morris, the question of creation versus evolution is ultimately one of two conflicting world views—one God centered and one focused upon Satan:

> we must stress once again that this question of creation or evolution is not merely a peripheral scientific issue, but rather is nothing less than the age-long conflict between God and Satan. There are only two basic world-views. One is a God-centered view of life and meaning and purpose—the other is a creature-centered view. Any educational system for the training of the coming generation must and will seek to inculcate one or the other. Any attempt to mediate or compromise between these two world-views will thus inevitably result in eventual capitulation of one of them, and this almost always will be in favor of the humanistic evolutionary system.[25]

Evolution and secular humanism are equated by Morris:

> Though modern evolutionism is essentially synonymous with humanism, which defies man, its real goal (and even this is coming more clearly into focus today, with the resurgence of astrology and other reforms of occultism) is nothing less than Satanism, which exalts Satan as god.[26]

Morris's equation of secular humanism and evolution is by no means unique. According to former congressman John Conlan and attorney John Whitehead, "Evolution has altered the course of history by shifting the base of moral absolutes from traditional theism to Secular humanism."[27] Similarly Tim LaHaye argues that evolution is the "primary foundation" upon which modern secular education is based.[28]

Creation science leaders clearly see themselves as challenging what they perceive to be the dominant model of evolution/secular humanism. They maintain that the evolutionists are in a defensive position whenever they are confronted by an alternative theory such as creationism. As Morris explains:

> When creationists propose, however, that creation be taught in the schools along with evolution, evolutionists commonly react emotionally, rather than scientifically. Their "religion" of naturalism and humanism has been in effect the established religion of the state for a hundred years and they fear competition.[29]

To some extent, the domination of science and education by the secular humanists is a result of ultra-fundamentalists having ignored science and focused their attention on evangelicalism and their faith:

> The real problem is that Christians have, for half a century (since the Scopes trial in particular), been concentrating on evangelism and "personal" Christianity, almost completely abandoning science and education to the evolutionary humanists.[30]

Morris argues that if creationists desire only the creationist model to be taught then they should send their children to private schools, and that if evolutionists only want evolution taught that they should do the same. Assuming that evolution is linked to the larger philosophical religious system of secular humanism, he maintains that the public schools should either be neutral and teach nothing or teach both. For him, this is the most equitable and constitutional approach.[31] According to Duane T. Gish, a colleague of Morris's at the Institute for Creation Research:

> To restrict the teaching concerning origins to a single theory, that of organic evolution, and to teach it as an established scientific fact, constitutes indoctrination in a humanistic religious philosophy. Such a procedure violates the Constitutional prohibition against the teaching of sectarian religious views just as clearly as if the teaching concerning origins were restricted to the Book of Genesis. In the spirit of fairness and of academic freedom we plead for a balanced presentation of all the evidence.[32]

Support for educational bills that would maintain a dual system of science instruction—i.e. creationism and evolution were introduced throughout the country during the early 1980s. This movement was led by Wendell Bird, a Yale Law School student and a creationist. In an award winning essay for the *Yale Law Journal*, Bird argued that teaching only evolution in the public schools violated the free exercise of religion guaranteed by the Constitution by forcing students to receive instruction that was heretical to their religious beliefs.[33] Basing his arguments on previous Supreme Court decisions such as those exempting Amish children from compulsory high school attendance and Jehovah's Witnesses being excused from classroom flag ceremonies, Bird developed the theory that evolutionary teaching unconstitutionally interfered with the religious beliefs of creationists. In addition, Bird maintained that the exclusive teaching of evolution compelled responses by students contrary to their personal and religious beliefs. Arguing the constitutional principle that the government may not restrict the rights of an individual more than is absolutely necessary in order to achieve its objectives, Bird maintained that the schools should "neutralize" their biology curriculum by teaching both evolution and scientific creationism.[34]

Drawing on the work of Morris and his colleagues at the Creation Science Research Center, Bird argued that a case for scientific creationism could be developed through the discussion of scientific empirical evidence, rather than religious beliefs. Bird's argument was based on the assumption that if scientific creationism could be shown to be a science, it could not be rejected as part of the curriculum because of its religious content.[35]

After finishing law school, Bird joined Morris at the Creation Science Research Center. Further refining his arguments, Bird made an extremely strong case for the interpretation that teaching only evolution was a violation of religious freedom. Revising a resolution first written by Morris in the early 1970s, Bird argued systematically that scientific creationism should be given equal time in the schools along with evolution, that only a "balanced treatment" was ultimately constitutionally acceptable.[36]

By mid-1979 thousands of copies of Bird's draft resolution were being circulated throughout the country. Bird's resolution became the basis for model legislation throughout the country. Although legislation failed in South Carolina, similar bills were subsequently introduced in eight state legislatures in 1980 and an additional fourteen legislatures in 1981.[37]

The most significant action taken concerning "balanced treatment" legislation occurred in Arkansas. On March 19, 1981, Governor Frank White signed into law a statute requiring "balanced treatment of creation and evolution science." Act 590 became a model for creationist legislation that was eventually introduced in at least twenty other states. Opposing the passage of the law, the American Civil Liberties Union took on the case for twenty-three plaintiffs, including a number of clergymen and religious organizations. They primarily challenged the law on the basis of the First Amendment Requirement of the Separation of Church and State.[38] William R. Overton, the United States District Judge who presided over the case, argued against the creationist forces maintaining that the Arkansas legislation represented a conscious attempt to introduce religious beliefs into the public school curriculum. According to Overton:

> The application and content of First Amendment principles are not determined by public opinion polls or by a majority vote. Whether the proponents of Act 590 constitute the majority or the minority is quite irrelevant under a constitutional system of government. No group, no matter how large or small, may use the organs of government, of which the public schools are the most conspicuous and influential, to foist its religious beliefs on others.[39]

Citing Justice Felix Frankfurter, Overton concluded his decision by quoting him to the effect that:

> "We renew our conviction that 'we have staked the very existence of our country on the faith that complete separation between the state and religion is best for the state and best for religion.' " *Everson v. Board of Education*, 330 U.S. at 59. If nowhere else, in the relation between Church and State, 'good fences make good neighbors.' " *McCollum v. Board of Education*, 333 U.S. 203,232 (1948).[40]

Arkansas was only the first skirmish in a much larger battle. Virtually simultaneous with the Arkansas decision Kelly Segraves, director of the Creation-Science Research Center filed a complaint in the names of his three children, all of whom were minors, in the Superior Court of Sacramento, California "aimed at correcting the philosophical imbalance regarding evolution and creationism in public education in California."[41] A week long trial was held in March of 1981. Although the state of California had over thirty witnesses prepared to defend the validity of evolutionary theory, the court declined to enter into a debate over the scientific virtues of either creationism or evolution. Instead, it focused its attention on the "anti-dogmatism policy" adopted by the state board of education in 1972. According to this policy:

> on the subject of discussing origins of life and earth in public schools:
> 1) dogmatism be changed to conditional statements where speculation is

offered as explanation for origin; and 2) science should emphasize "how" and not "ultimate cause" for origin.[42]

On June 12, 1981, Judge Irving H. Perluss ruled that the state board of education had taken no actions that interfered with the plaintiffs free exercise of religion. At the same time, it directed the California State Board of Education to reiterate its antidogmatism policy and that science instruction not be presented as possessing a set of absolute answers.[43]

Attempts to establish "equal time" provisions for creationist instruction were introduced into the Louisiana legislature shortly after the appearance of the previously discussed creationist legislation in Arkansas. A "balanced model" of instruction was required to go into effect in the fall of 1983. Challenged on constitutional grounds, the procreationist legislation that was introduced at this time has gone through numerous challenges by the American Civil Liberties Union and others.[44] By December of 1986, the case had made its way to the Supreme Court.


## CRITICISMS OF THE CREATION-SCIENCE MODEL

Murray Gell-Mann, a 1969 Nobel Prize Winner for Physics, in an editorial criticizing Louisiana's statute mandating the teaching of "creation science," argued that:

> the portion of science that is attacked by such statutes is far more extensive than many people realize, embracing important parts of physics, chemistry, astronomy, and geology as well as many of the central ideas of biology and anthropology. In particular, the notion of reducing the age of the earth by a factor of nearly a million and that of the expanding universe by an even larger factor, conflicts in the most basic way with numerous robust conclusions of physical science. For example, fundamental and well-established principles of nuclear physics are challenged for no sound reason, when 'creation scientists' attack the validity of the radioactive clocks that provide the most reliable methods used to date the earth.[45]

Gell-Mann argues that creation science, if imposed on the public schools, would make students ill-prepared to deal with problems of health, agriculture, industrial production, environmental quality and national defense. Half in jest, Gellman asks whether or not we want the disposal of nuclear wastes to follow the principles of creationist nuclear physics, or oil exploration based on creationist geological time schemes.[46]

According to Gell-Mann, attempts to impose creation science on American public education closely parallels the situation in the Soviet Union under Stalin when the authorities interfered with the teaching of biology by insisting that the pseudo-scientific theories of Lysenko be followed, rather than more substantive scientific approaches. The negative consequences for the development of agriculture and teaching and research in general have been widely documented. Creation science poses a similar threat. According to Gell-Mann, all scientific discoveries are subject to revision with new discoveries or when contrary but convincing arguments arise:

> By contrast, "creation scientists" who are members of the Creation Research Society have to subscribe to a statement that begins as follows: "(1) The Bible is the Written word of God, and because we believe it to be inspired throughout, all of its assertions are historically and scientifically true in all of the original autographs. To the student of nature this means that the account of the origins in Genesis is a factual presentation of simple historical truths. (2) All basic types of living things, including man were made by direct creative acts of God during creation Week as described in Genesis. Whatever biological changes have occured since creation accomplished changes only within the original created kinds."[47]

Gell-Mann points out that the Creationists are putting forward a model of science which instead of being based upon observation is based upon religious faith.[48] Ultimately he concludes that the "Fundamentalists have a perfect right to their beliefs but no right to control the teaching of science in the public schools."[49]

In an article commenting on the case of *Segraves et al. v. State of California et al.*, Harvey Siegel—a philosopher of science and education—argues that the public schools:

> in favoring evolutionary theory over creationism in the science curriculum, is not failing to be neutral. It is not being biased or unfairly favoring the former over the latter, for there are exceedingly strong reasons for favoring evolutionary theory. *It meets the disciplinary standards of science; creationism does not.*[50]

According to Siegel, the state cannot be expected to remain:

> philosophically neutral...if "neutrality" is construed as nonjudgemental. For to be nonjudgemental by failing to distinguish science from pseudoscience in the science curriculum is to fail to maintain standards of disciplinary adequacy.[51]

Siegel goes on to maintain that the religious freedom of the creationists is only violated if an individual is not allowed to acknowledge his or her religious belief in either speech or action. However, a science course that rejects creationism as an answer to questions concerning the origins of life does not violate the religious rights of students or punish them. Instead, according to Siegel:

It simply maintains standards of scientific adequacy and lets students know that creationists fail to meet minimum scientific standards. To the extent that a student's religious beliefs contradict good science, the science teacher has an obligation to point that out to the student.[52]

Siegel emphasizes that of course the science teacher may not force a student to abandon his or her religious beliefs for a scientific interpretation, but only that religious belief does not constitute good science.[53]

## THE SUPREME COURT AND LOUISIANA'S CREATIONISM LAW

Louisiana's creation-science statute was overturned by the Supreme Court in a decision made June 19, 1987. According to their ruling, requiring public school instruction in Creationism as a counter balance to instruction in evolutionary biology represented a promotion of religion and therefore was an infringement on First Amendment rights.[54] The decision was seven-to-two. According to the Court's majority, Louisiana's creation-science statute was:

facially invalid as violative of the Establishment Clause of the First Amendment, because it lacks a clear secular purpose.... (a) The Act does not further its stated purpose of "protecting academic freedom." It does not enhance the freedom of teachers to teach what they choose and fails to further the goal of "teaching all of the evidence." Forbidding the teaching of evolution when creation-science is not also taught undermines the provision of a scientific comprehensive education. Moreover, requiring the teaching of creation science with evolution does not give school-teachers a flexibility that they did not already possess to supplant the present science curriculum with the presentation of theories, besides evolution about the origin of life.[55]

The Court further maintained in its decision that the Act's contention that it promoted "a basic concept of fairness" by requiring the teaching of all of the evidence on a subject was without merit. According to the Court:

the Act evinces a discriminatory preference for the teaching of creation science and against the teaching of evolution by requiring that curriculum guides be developed and research services supplied for teaching creationism but not for teaching evolution, by limiting membership on the research service panels to "creation scientists," and by forbidding school boards to discriminate against anyone who "chooses to be a creation-scientist" or to teach creation science, while failing to protect those who choose to teach other theories or who refuse to teach creation science.[56]

According to the Court:

A law intended to maximize the comprehensiveness and effectiveness of science instruction would encourage the teaching of all scientific theories about human origins.[57]

Instead, the Louisiana Creation-Science Act had the effect of discrediting evolution as a theory by counter-balancing its theories whenever possible with the teaching of creation-science.[58]

Critical to the Court's arguments was its further contention that the Louisiana creation-science law endorsed religion by advancing the religious belief that a supernatural being created life. According to the Court:

The Act's primary purpose was to change the public school science curriculum to provide persuasive advantage to a particular religious doctrine that rejects the factual basis of evolution in its entirety. Thus, the Act is designed *either* to promote the theory of creation science that embodies a particular religious tenet *or* to prohibit the teaching of a scientific theory disfavored by certain religious sects. In either case, the Act violates the First Amendment.[59]

The Louisiana Creation-Science Act, according to the Court's interpretation, lacked balance and fairness. The purpose of its enactment was to promote the religious viewpoint that a supernatural being had created life. In doing so, the act violated the First Amendment of the Constitution and was stricken down.

The recent, and on-going attempts of ultra-fundamentalist groups to introduce a balanced science curriculum into the public schools, which includes both instruction in evolution and creationism, represent in my opinion a well-calculated strategy for focusing the general public's attention on their cause. Edward Larson has pointed out that since the *Scopes* trial, people on both sides of the case aimed their arguments beyond the court to the general public.[60] In much the same way, the recent court cases in Arkansas, California and Louisiana have had the purpose of bringing the creationists, and more generally the ultra-fundamentalists', beliefs to the attention of the general public. In doing so, the Creationism controversy and the creationists' demands for a "balanced curriculum" should be understood in the context of a much larger battle for control of the public schools and the culture at large. The extent to which this is true can be seen in Chapter Five which deals with "The Family and Education."

# Chapter Five

# The Family and Education

⚬

At the heart of the ultra-fundamentalist critique of public education is a belief that the institution of the American family is under attack. "Profamily" activists protest the right of women to terminate a pregnancy (legalized abortion), and the equal rights of women and homosexuals as guaranteed by the Equal Rights Amendment. They have also charged that the public schools are exercising what they believe to be undo interference in the family's right to educate and rear its children. The teaching of evolution, sex education and values clarification courses, the use of textbooks emphasizing "secular humanist" values, and the prohibition of school prayer are all seen as evidence of this phenomenon.

David Bollier has argued that the ultra-fundamentalists have used the "family" as a vehicle to focus attention on issues that are of greatest concern to them. According to him, the profamily movement is simply a way of packaging the ultra-fundamentalist agenda for social change in a highly emotional package. Bollier notes that Phyllis Schafly, for example, claims that the traditional American family will be destroyed if the Equal Rights Amendment is passed; and according to Jerry Falwell, the homosexual population is interested primarily in recruiting children to follow their sexual practices.[1]

## EDUCATION AND THE STATE BEING PERCEIVED AS A THREAT TO THE RIGHTS OF THE FAMILY

The profamily activists question the State's right to interfere with the traditional role and function of the family. In this context Onalee McGraw of the Heritage Foundation maintains that:

Those who believe in objective values are being forced to submit their children to value-inculcation that is at total variance with their own beliefs. If no directive from the school authorities is issued to say that this kind of behavior is simply not permitted, the school is inculcating the concept that how one conducts oneself is merely a matter of taste. Self-expression is judged to be of greater worth than self-restraint, modesty or consideration for the sensitivities of others.[2]

For ultra-fundamentalists like McGraw, America society has been going through a cultural crisis unprecedented in our history—one in which the public schools are no longer recognized by many people as serving an appropriate or suitable function:

Can there be any doubt that the past decade has generated the most pervasive and widespread dissatisfaction with the present state-supported school system since its establishment? The public no longer accepts the premise that the state school, in addition to the home and the church, is the best vehicle through which American children must be socialized to be adjusted and productive participants in the "American way of life."[3]

While the question of what should be the role and function of the public schools is being debated, McGraw maintains that traditional interest groups are deliberately working to increase and expand their control of the public schools. McGraw believes that the House Education and Labor Committee, the Senate Human Resources Committees, vested interest groups in the education sector such as the American Federation of Teachers and the National Education Association, various educational think tanks, university departments of education, and the federal bureaucracy and their clientele have joined together to "represent an educational establishment that continues to hold the upper hand over education consumers."[4]

According to McGraw and other ultra-fundamentalists such as Tim LaHaye and Barbara Morris, parental involvement in the schools has become more circumscribed in recent years. Since the early 1960s local school boards have lost much of their control of the decision-making process as control of public education has increasingly shifted to the federal bureaucracy. Through groups such as the National Institute of Education, the National Science Foundation and the National Endowment for the Humanities, prestige, funding and power have been assigned to various individuals and institutions to implement their educational goals and objectives in local schools.[5]

Federal encroachment into the local control of schools has been equated by the ultra-fundamentalists with the imposition of a state controlled religion upon the culture:

> Is it conceivable that America could institute a state-controlled religion? The foundation is already being laid. Until 1979, we did not have a tax-supported religion in America. Instead, all religions were free to operate within the framework of minimal legal guidelines. But that changed in 1979, for during that year, under the guidance of a well publicized born-again president, the federal government established a Department of Education with a $40 million budget. Since the educational system has been taken over by humanism, and since humanism is an officially declared religion, we find the government establishing a religion and giving the high priest a position in the president's cabinet.[6]

Barbara Morris maintains that with the imposition of federal policies onto local school districts, local control is a "fantasy." According to her, groups such as the National Science Foundation and the National Endowment of the Humanities contract with "change agent curriculum developers" to create curriculums such as the "infamous" *Man: A Course of Study* (MACOS).[7]

It is important to note that Morris equates the introduction of federal education programs such as the Elementary and Secondary Education Act (ESEA) of 1965 with the introduction of "federally funded change agent programs and curricula."[8] Such programs, according to Morris, are deliberate attempts to change the existing power structure within the culture. Children are a primary target in this change process:

> Children are to be changed for a particular purpose with a particular goal in mind. When the federal government spends millions of dollars to train "leaders of educational change" it is obvious the purpose is not to perpetuate the status quo. The purpose is to satisfy the desire of the government to amass power and control in order to facilitate the Humanist new world order. And how could any of it be done without the government school curriculum?[9]

Funding at the federal level goes only to those groups or institutions who facilitate change. Teachers are transformed by the federal programs into "zealous missionary change agents."[10] Programs such as the National Diffusion Network, which was set up by the federal government to disseminate innovative educational ideas is seen as a deliberately created instrument of social change. Barbara Morris asks her readers in *Change Agents in the Schools*:

Do you understand the significance of this National Diffusion Network? It means that an elite corps of 22 change agents in Washington decide what federal programs will be promoted and disseminated throughout the schools—government and nongovernment alike. The 22 change agents, who are chosen '...for their ability to analyze the effectiveness of educational programs' have the power to select and fund, without benefit of public participation or parental involvement, without any account-ability—what programs will go into the schools.[11]

While arguing that not all of the programs disseminated by the National Diffusion Network are necessarily bad, the ultra-fundamentalists none-theless believe that they represent the beginning of the creation "of a totally nationalized school system."[12]

Criticisms of federal involvement in education—particularly in the context of the profamily movement—represent the continuation of a complex constitutional debate that extends back to the 1920s and the Supreme Court case of *Pierce v. Society of the Sisters of the Holy Names of Jesus and Mary*.[13] Under a statewide compulsory education act passed in Oregon, parents were required to send their children "to a public school for the period of time a public school shall be held during the current year."[14] As a result of the law, children were withdrawn from private schools such as the one run by the Society of Sisters. Objections were raised. Cases filed at the state level ruled in favor of the state officials and their compulsory attendance law. When the case was appealed, however, the Supreme Court indicated that only limited tolerance would be given to the state's interfering with the parent's control of their children's educa-tion. As the Supreme Court explained:

> In this day and under our civilization, the child of man is his parent's child and not the state's....It is not seriously debatable that the parental right to guide one's child intellectually and religiously is a most substantial part of the liberty and freedom of the parent.[15]

The decision went on to state that:

> The fundamental theory of liberty upon which all government is based in this Union excludes any general power of the state to standardize its children by forcing them to accept instruction from public teachers only. The child is not the mere creature of the state; those who nurture him and direct his destiny have the right coupled with the high duty, to recognize and prepare him for additional obligations.[16]

Unless a child is abused or mistreated by an act of omission or commission, it is not the place of the state to interfere with the education of a child.

Steven Arons in his article "The Separation of Church and State: *Pierce* Reconsidered," argues that in *Pierce*, and subsequent Supreme Court decisions such as *West Virginia v. Barnett* and *Wisconsin v. Yoder*, demonstrate that education by its very nature involves the inculcation of values and beliefs. There is no way that education can avoid this fact. Decisions such as *Pierce v. Society of Sisters* "leaves unsettled the question of just where in the area between absolute parental control and complete state control the Supreme Court will place the limits of allowable state regulation of schooling."[17] This issue is an extraordinarily difficult one to resolve—especially when considering sex education in the schools.

## THE PROFAMILY MOVEMENT AND SEX EDUCATION

Sex education is viewed by many ultra-fundamentalists such as Barbara Morris as simply an extension of values education. Specifically, through the use of techniques such as values clarification, role playing and group discussion:

> the purpose of sex education is to eradicate Christian values and Christian behavior relating to sexual activity and to replace them with Humanist values and behavior.[18]

Tim LaHaye maintains that sex education has proved to be a catastrophic failure. Instead of decreasing unwanted pregnancies and venereal diseases, he claims that these conditions have in fact increased enormously since sex education was introduced into the public schools.[19]

A legitimate question arises as to what rights parents have in determining where, how and what their children will learn of a subject as sensitive as sex education. Many of the ultra-fundamentalists argue that sexual values pervade the entire curriculum, so that even if a parent withdraws his or her child from sex education classes, the topic still makes its way into other subjects included in the curriculum.

In the case of *Citizens for Parental Rights v. San Mateo Board of Education* (124 Cal. Rptr. 68 (1975) ) parents protesting sex education courses argued that their children had been pressured informally to attend sex education courses and that this pressure ultimately represented an infringement on their religious freedom. According to this lower court decision:

a mere personal difference of opinion as to the curriculum which is taught in our public schools system does not give rise to a constitutional right in the private citizen to control exposure to knowledge.[20]

Clearly, what is at work in cases such as this is a conflict between basic value systems put forward by the schools and those of a select group within the community. In fact, Constitutional precedents clearly seem to support the notion that parents do have the right to determine what it is that their children should or should not learn in the schools. For example, in *Wisconsin v. Yoder*, the issue of compulsory attendance was challenged by a group of Amish parents: compulsory education beyond the eighth grade level infringed upon their religious beliefs. According to the *Yoder* decision:

> a State's interest in universal education, however highly we rank it, is not totally free from a balancing process when it impinges on the fundamental rights and interests, such as those specifically protected by the Free Exercise Clause of the First Amendment, and the traditional interest of parents with respect to the religious upbringing of their children so long as they, in the words of *Pierce*, "prepare (them) for additional obligations."[21]

The problem, of course, is how the rights of all parties are to be maintained, particularly if contradictory values are held by the individuals involved. Another example is when the issue of homosexual rights and education is addressed.

## HOMOSEXUALITY, EDUCATION, AND THE PROFAMILY MOVEMENT

Homosexuality is viewed by the ultra-fundamentalists as a major threat to the family and American culture in general. Throughout their literature, reference is made to the threat posed by homosexuals as an organized interest group. In fact, Tim LaHaye suggests that the counter offensive mounted against Anita Bryant's attack on homosexual teachers in Dade County, Florida during the mid-1970s, may have contributed significantly to the reemergence of ultra-fundamentalists as a political force. In his book *The Battle for the Public Schools*, LaHaye explains that:

> The homosexual and media attacks on Anita Bryant and the good people of Dade County, Florida, forced many people to awaken to the seriousness of the situation.[22]

For the ultra-fundamentalists, homosexuality represents a direct attack on the American family. By maintaining the rights of homosexuals as citizens, ultra-fundamentalist teachers such as Jerry Falwell are afraid that the government will undermine the foundations of our culture and society. In a fund-raising letter dated February 15, 1982, Falwell wrote, for example, that he felt that the:

> Courts and the laws of our land will come to officially legitimatize perversion and perverted acts and the very foundations of moral principle upon which this great nation was established may soon crumble.[23]

Rejecting the notion that the homosexual community can exercise its sexual preferences and let others do as they see fit, ultra-fundamentalists leaders such as Falwell believe that the homosexual community is interested in perverting the minds and belief systems of American youth:

> We must stop the homosexuals dead in their tracks—before they get one step further towards warping the minds of our youth!... The enemy is in our camp! And they are after the most prized possession—our children![24]

The ultra-fundamentalists consider homosexual teachers to be unfit to work with children. No consideration is given to the teachers' rights. It is assumed that if they are Gay that they will try to influence the children they teach to follow their own sexual preferences.

Such an attitude is an obvious violation of the civil rights of the homosexual teacher. Inappropriate sexual behavior is a cause for dismissal and possible criminal charges for heterosexual teachers and homosexual teachers. To assume that homosexual teachers are going to "pervert" their students is no more appropriate or fair than to assume that heterosexual teachers will do the same. Yet, given the basic beliefs of the ultra-fundamentalists, no other assumption is possible. For ultra-fundamentalist leaders like Jerry Falwell, "the entire homosexual movement is an indictment against America and is contributing to its ultimate downfall."[25]

The question then arises: If a parent objects to having his or her child taught by a homosexual teacher, does the parent have the right to withdraw the child from the teacher's class? What if the teacher objects? Whose rights should predominate? According to Falwell:

> God considers the sin of homosexuality as abominable. He destroyed the cities of Sodom and Gomorrah because of their involvement in this sin.

The Old Testament law is clear concerning this issue: "Thou shat not lie with mankind, as with womankind, it is abomination" (Lev. 18:22)[26]

Within such a believe system, clearly there can be no compromise—constitutional or otherwise.

## FAMILY CHOICE OR STATE CONTROL IN EDUCATION?

Jerry Falwell has argued that:

The most important function performed by the family is the rearing and character formation of children, a function it was uniquely created to perform and for which no remotely adequate substitute has been found. The family is the best and most efficient "department of health, education and welfare."[27]

For ultra-fundamentalists such as Falwell, the right to educate one's children is a right granted to them by God and not by the Courts or the State.

The question of family choice in education has received considerable attention from scholars in recent years. Particularly noteworthy is John E. Coons and Stephen D. Sugarman's *Education by Choice: The Case for Family Control.*[28] Coons and Sugarman provide a detailed examination of the issue of who should have control over the education of children, the family or professional educators acting as agents of the state? In his foreword to the book, the sociologist James S. Coleman argues that the debate concerning family choice in education:

reflects a division on very deeply held values, involving beliefs about the proper division of authority between the state and the family, beliefs about the dangers to social cohesion of deviant doctrines, beliefs about the relative abilities of professionals and their clients to decide what is best, and beliefs in the importance of maintaining the existing institutional order.[29]

Ultimately, it is this issue—the reality of widely conflicting values and beliefs within American society—that is the basis for the conflict involving the ultra-fundamentalists and the public schools.

Coons and Sugarman begin their book by posing what is the key question that must be addressed when considering the relationship between the ultra-fundamentalists and American education. Specifically, they ask the reader to:

Imagine a people aspiring to live in harmony, to cooperate in production and defense, and to distribute society's rewards in a just manner. Suppose, however, that they are divided a dozen ways about the nature of the good life—some valuing personal striving and acquisition, others pleasure, others quiet and the life of the spirit. How would such a people design the education of their people?[30]

As Coons and Sugarman explain, the question is an important one, for the society described is the United States. America, while certainly a nation—and perhaps even a people of sorts—"is a virtual menagerie."[31]

According to Coons and Sugarman, despite the superficial sameness resulting from the country's industrial economy, there is no identifiable American ethic, or if it does exist, "it is passing."[32] Contemporary America is defined as much by its pluralism as any other single factor. In such a pluralistic society there is no longer a clear and unified set of values that can be used as the basis for defining the goals and purpose of public education.

Coons and Sugarman maintain that the range and number of choices open to parents in terms of educating their children in the public schools is far too narrow. According to them, the family, rather than the state, should be given the ultimate power to make educational decisions in the child's best interest. Through the implementation of family subsidies (various types of vouchers and tuition tax credits), they propose to offer a much wider-range of choice than is currently available from the public school system in the United States.

It is clear that there are no easy answers to the issue of state versus family control of public education. It is an extremely complex debate with rights and duties claimed by both the private individual and the state. In Chapter Six, "School Prayer and the State Control of Christian Schools," the same issue is raised in the context of the debate over whether or not the state should restrict prayer in the schools and what restrictions and regulations the state can legitimately impose upon private schooling.

# Chapter Six

# School Prayer and State Regulation of Christian Schools

A number of ultra-fundamentalist critics maintain that the rights of Christians are being circumscribed by the direct intervention of the state in the matter of prayer in the public schools and in the regulation of private schools. In fact, a reasonable argument can be made that since the early 1960s state and federal governmental agencies have intervened in both these areas in ways that have significantly diminished the latitude and freedom afforded to ultra-fundamentalist groups. Nowhere is this more evident than in the case of the restrictions that have been placed on prayer and Bible reading in the public schools.

## ULTRA-FUNDAMENTALISM AND THE SCHOOL PRAYER DEBATE

The appropriateness of prayer in the public schools has become one of the most emotional issues raised by the ultra-fundamentalists as part of their recent educational crusade. For them, returning prayer to the public schools is absolutely necessary if American society is to overcome its problems. According to Ed McAteer, president of the Religious Roundtable:

> If we are to stem the tide of lawlessness, drug addiction, and sexual perversion which adversely affect academic performance, we must start with putting God back into our school systems.[1]

75

The nationally syndicated television evangelist James Robison maintains that "the assassinations [of public figures]...acceleration of the Vietnam War, escalation of crime, disintegration of families, racial conflict, teenage pregnancies and venereal disease" can all be ascribed "to the Supreme Court's ban on mandatory school prayer."[2]

Once again, secular humanism is blamed for removing prayer from the public schools. Referring to the supposed domination of the schools by secular humanist thinkers and educators, Tim LaHaye argues that:

> Because of them prayer, Bible reading, Bible study, released time classes, Easter, and Christmas celebrations have been eliminated. Easter has been changed to "spring break," Christmas to "winter vacation." Christmas programs can feature Santa, Rudolph and Scrooge—but not the One whose entrance into the world we are celebrating.[3]

Whether or not prayer and Bible reading should be allowed in the public schools is ultimately a Constitutional question—one based primarily on the interpretation of the Establishment clause of the First Amendment to the Constitution, which states that "Congress shall make no law respecting an establishment of religion, or prohibiting the free exercise thereof."

The framers of the Constitution, contrary to the arguments of many ultra-fundamentalists, were reluctant to introduce the question of religion into the Constitution and the government which it formed. Hundreds of years of religious strife in Europe, combined together with the diversity of religious beliefs and background among the Colonists, had led leaders such as John Adams to conclude that if the issue was not mentioned both religion and the state would be best served. Adams hoped that: "Congress will never meddle with religion further than to say their own prayers, and to fast and to give thanks once a year."[4]

Although no general religious provision was included in the Constitution itself, provisions were made to prohibit states from requiring a religious test in order for a person to serve in a political office. When the Constitution was approved by the states, six states ratified the document, while at the same time proposing amendments guaranteeing religious freedom. Two states, North Carolina and Rhode Island refused to ratify the Constitution until a Bill of Rights that included clauses guaranteeing religious freedom was included. In 1789, James Madison after considerable consultation and discussion, introduced into the House of Representatives a compilation of proposals for amendments. These amendments, which were to eventually become the Bill of Rights, emphasized the Separation of Church and State, guaranteed religious freedom and prohibited the establishment of a state sponsored religion.[5]

The First Amendment has been the foundation for all subsequent interpretations concerning the role of religion and education in American society. In 1947, for example, the Supreme Court used the First Amendment in *Everson v. Board of Education*[6] as the basis for formulating a general policy that has dominated constitutional thinking ever since:

> The "establishment of religion" clause of the First Amendment means at least this: Neither a state nor the Federal Government can set up a church. Neither can pass laws which aid one religion, aid all religions, or prefer one religion over another....No tax in any amount, large or small, can be levied to support by religious activities or institutions, whatever they may be called, or whatever form they may adopt to teach or practice religion. Neither a state nor the Federal Government can, openly or secretly, participate in the affairs of any religious organizations or groups and vice versa. In the words of Jefferson, the clause against establishment of religion by law was intended to erect "a wall of separation between Church and State."[7]

This interpretation has been reaffirmed in subsequent Supreme Court cases involving School Prayer and Bible Reading.

Prior to 1962, at least twelve states permitted or required prayer and Bible reading in the public schools. The general attitude of the courts was that the Bible and general prayer were not sectarian, and therefore did not violate the provisions of the First Amendment. In 1962 in *Engel v. Vitale*, however, the Supreme Court found the recitation of a prayer developed for use in the public schools by the New York Regents unconstitutional.[8] In *Engel v. Vitale* the court argued that just because a prayer is denominationally neutral and voluntary does not mean that it is excluded from the limitations imposed by the Establishment Clause of the First Amendment. According to the Court:

> The Establishment Clause, unlike the Free Exercise Clause, does not depend upon any showing of direct governmental compulsion and is violated by the enactment of laws which establish an official religion whether those laws operate directly to coerce non-observing individuals or not.[9]

A year later in *School District of Abington Township v. Schempp and Murray v. Curlett*[10] two separate cases were reviewed by the Court, in which it was decided that enforced Bible reading and school prayer violated both the First and the Fourteenth Amendments to the Constitution. As part of this decision, it was explicitly argued by the Court that it could not:

accept that the concept of neutrality, which does not permit a State to require a religious exercise even with the consent of the majority of those affected, collides with the majority's right to the exercise of free religion. While the Free Exercise Clause clearly prohibits the use of state action to deny the rights of free exercise to *anyone*, it has never meant that a majority could use the machinery of the State to practice its beliefs.[11]

Continuing its argument, the Court maintained that in relationship "between man and religion, the State is firmly committed to the position of neutrality." A position "clearly and concisely stated in the words of the First Amendment."[12]

In May of 1982, President Ronald Reagan put forward a proposed Constitutional Amendment that would permit so-called voluntary school prayer. The wording of the proposed amendment read:

> Nothing in the Constitution shall be construed to prohibit individual or group prayer in public schools or other public institutions. No person shall be required by the United States or by any state to participate in prayer.[13]

Some legislators, such as Senator John Danforth, consider government-mandated voluntary prayer a contradiction in terms. He has proposed that "voluntary" be defined to include any prayer "composed, prescribed, directed, supervised, or organized by an official employee of a state or local government agency, including public school principals or teachers."[14]

Reagan's efforts failed. In May of 1984 his proposed amendment was defeated in the Senate. In its place the "equal access" act was passed, which allows students to meet for philosophical, religious and political purposes as part of an extracurricular activity. Whether or not students have the constitutional right to meet under such circumstances is being tested by the Supreme Court. In *Bender v. Williamsport Area School District* (October 15, 1985) the issue is being debated as to whether or not the First Amendment clause prohibits a student-initiated prayer group from getting together in school during a student activity period.[15]

Conservative political critics such as George Will have raised the question of whether or not including prayer in the public schools is in fact going to best serve the needs of religion:

> [T]he question is: is public-school prayer apt to serve authentic religion, or is it apt to be mere attitudinizing, a thin gruel of vague religious vocabulary? According to some polls, more Americans favor prayers in school than regularly pray in church. Supermarkets sell processed cheese and instant mashed potatoes, so many Americans must like bland

substitutes for the real thing. But it is one thing for the nation's palate to tolerate frozen waffles; it is another and more serious thing for the nation's soul to be satisfied with add-water-and-stir religiosity. When government acts as liturgist for a pluralistic society, the result is bound to be a puree that is tasteless, in several senses.[16]

Another political conservative, James Kilpatrick, raises the question of why the ultra-fundamentalists are pushing so hard for the inclusion of prayer in the schools. As he comments:

Isn't it ironic that folks who quake at the danger of "secular humanism" are the very ones pushing for prayer in the public schools, an ultimate secularization.[17]

Why, in fact, are the ultra-fundamentalists so concerned with the school prayer issue? The removal of prayer and Bible reading from the public schools during the early 1960s was seen as a clear demonstration of the increasing secularization of the society. The removal of school prayer was seen as the first step in a series of efforts to impose state control on individuals—limiting them in their right to practice their religious beliefs. In a recent federal court case involving textbooks and their content, ultra-fundamentalists have argued that at least fifty of the 4,000 textbooks used in the Mobile, Alabama public schools unconstitutionally suppress the role of religion in American society and advance the teachings of secular humanism.

### Smith v. Board of School Commissioners (1987)

In *Smith v. Board of School Commissioners*, 624 evangelical Christians filed a suit against state and local education officials in Alabama arguing that the Mobile public schools promoted the religion of secular humanism. According to the plaintiffs, the public schools promoted the godless religion of secular humanism while inhibiting the God-Centered religions of Christianity and Judaism.

People for the American Way, an anticensorship group in Washington, D.C. headed by the television producer Norman Lear, underwrote many of the legal expenses for lawyers opposing the case of the plaintiffs. People for the American Way interpreted the case as being one in which conservative religious groups were trying to restrict the content of textbooks being used in the schools. Ultra-fundamentalist leaders such as Phyllis Schafly, however, interpreted the case not as one of censorship, but one demanding that:

the 1st Amendment treats all religions alike. If Christianity and Judaism are disdained in public schools, Humanism should get the cold shoulder, too.[18]

Drawing on research conducted by Professor Paul Vitz of New York University (sponsored by the National Institute of Education), regarding the content of contemporary textbooks, the plaintiffs argued that the textbooks used in the Mobile, Alabama public schools consistently ignored the discussion of religious values. According to Vitz in his book *Censorship: Evidence of Bias in Our Children's Textbooks*, which is based on his National Institute of Education study: Religion, traditional family values, and conservative political and economic values have been reliably excluded from children's textbooks.[19]

Vitz argues that while there is no evidence of any conscious conspiracy operating to exclude religious materials from contemporary textbooks, the fact remains that a secular and liberal mindset pervades the educational and publishing world that is responsible for the elimination of these materials from school texts.[20]

Vitz looked at a total of sixty representative social studies textbooks used in grades one through four throughout the country. None of the textbooks was found to "contain one word referring to any religious activity in contemporary life."[21] No text referred to any child or adult praying. No text made reference to a church or synagogue. Texts used at the fifth and sixth grade level followed the same general pattern, as well as secondary school texts.[22] Vitz makes a very convincing case in his research for his argument at the conclusion of the book that:

> public school textbooks commonly exclude the history, heritage, beliefs, and values of millions of Americans. Those who believe in the traditional family are not represented. Those who believe in free enterprise are not represented. Those whose politics are conservative are almost unrepresented. Above all, those who are committed to their religious tradition—at the very least as an important part of the historical record—are not represented.[23]

While the exclusion of religious materials from textbooks can be explained in part by textbook publishers trying to avoid controversies involving the Separation of Church and State, a convincing argument emerges supporting the case of the ultra-fundamentalists.

It was the contention of the plaintiffs that the textbooks being used represented a comprehensive view of the world based upon the philosophy of Secular Humanism. The Court agreed ruling that:

> teaching that moral choices are purely personal and can only be based on some autonomous, as yet undiscovered and unfulfilled, inner self is a sweeping fundamental belief that must not be promoted by the public schools.... With these books, the State of Alabama has overstepped its mark, and must withdraw to perform it proper nonreligious functions.[24]

The ruling made in favor of the plaintiffs by Judge Brevard Hand was overturned by the federal appeals court in Cincinnati in August of 1987. According to the Cincinnati court, it could find no evidence that the plaintiff required children attending the Mobile schools "to affirm or deny a religious belief." The Cincinnati court rebuked Judge Hand for turning the First Amendment requirement that government be neutral about religion into "an affirmative obligation to speak about religion."[25] A lawyer representing the plaintiffs dismissed the Cincinnati court decision saying that the decision was simply "a whistle stop" on the way to the Supreme Court. The case was, in fact, denied for review by the Supreme Court in 1988 together with the Hawkins County case.

While the ultra-fundamentalists have consistently tried to encroach upon the authority and prerogatives of the public schools, it can be argued equally well that the fundamentalists see themselves as having their rights and freedoms encroached upon by state authorities in the control and regulation of private Christian schools.

## STATE REGULATION OF CHRISTIAN SCHOOLS

Christian day schools have expanded faster since the 1960s than any other segment of private education. Approximately eight to ten thousand of these schools have been established since the middle of the 1960s, with a total enrollment of about one million students.[26] The growth of the Christian day schools can be explained by the increasing dissatisfaction of conservative Christians with the academic and social environments of the public schools, as well as because of their belief that the schools have become increasingly secularized.[27] The exclusion of religious content from instruction, prohibitions against school prayer and the promotion of values and beliefs that are perceived as being anti-Christian have all contributed to the rapid growth of Christian day schools.[28] Rejection of public education in favor of private instruction on the part of evangelicals and more conservative Protestant groups represents a more broadly based criticism of American culture and society. According to James Carper:

for many evangelicals the public school exemplifies the trend they deplore in the changing American social order, such as uncertainty concerning sources of authority, dissolution of standards, waning of the Judeo-Christian value system, loosening of custom and constraint, scientism and governmental social engineering.[29]

Private Christian day schools are perceived as providing an environment for parents and their children in which traditional values can be nurtured and supported.

For ultra-fundamentalists such as Rousas Rushdoony, allowing Christian children to attend public schools is to deny Christ. As he explains:

> To surrender our children to anti-Christian, humanistic schools is to deny Christ. It is a greater evil than putting our children into modernist Sunday Schools and churches. A church after all, "commands" only two or three hours of child's time a week, whereas the state schools literally command our children five full days a week, if we submit them to this modern Moloch.[30]

For the ultra-fundamentalists education is inherently religious. Any state involvement with the schools is ultimately seen as a threat to the integrity of religious belief. Among many ultra-fundamentalists there is a widely held belief that state educational systems are hostile to the mission of the Christian schools. When attempts are made by agencies such as state departments of education to regulate Christian schools in areas such as curriculum and teacher certification, many ultra-fundamentalists assume that this is being done in order to limit their growth and development.

Some ultra-fundamentalists have likened the attempts of state boards of education to regulate Christian schools to the Greeks using the Trojan Horse to secretly enter the city of Troy in order to defeat the Trojan army. In much the same way, state boards of education attempting to regulate Christian schools, are seen as a subterfuge whereby the state can deflect the true mission of the religious schools to comply with their own secular purposes. As Alan Grover has explained in reference to the state of Ohio's Minimum Standards law, which outlines basic state requirements for public and private schools:

> The Minimum Standards are similar to the Trojan Horse. The very name sounds harmless. The volume containing the standards is externally attractive. We are told that following the Minimum Standards is the path to quality schools, and everyone is for quality schools. But what is inside? Is the material on the inside of such a nature as to allow a church operated

school, and more particularly, a Christian school, to embrace this document without sustaining irreparable damages.[31]

For Grover, Christian schools cannot comply with the requirements of Ohio's Minimum Standards "without destroying thereby their purpose for existence."[32] The requirements are perceived as being a violation of religious freedom.

State education agencies use a number of arguments to justify their regulation of private schools. These include seeing that students are provided with minimally competent individuals to instruct them, that basic standards of health and safety are complied with and so on. In addition, the State has a strong interest in seeing that its citizens are provided with basic skills in literacy and the fundamentals of a democratic political system.

The Supreme Court in cases such as *Wisconsin v. Yoder* (1972), *Everson v. Board of Education* (1947), *Pierce v. Society of Sisters* (1925) has repeatedly recognized the right of the state to regulate educational institutions.[33] In the case of *Pierce v. Society of Sisters,* for example, while the state was prohibited from interfering with a private Catholic school's basic curriculum, it could require that a basic secular education be provided along with the school's regular programs. According to the decision in *Pierce*:

> There are five predominant policies behind nonpublic regulation: (1) to reinforce school attendance requirements, (2) to prevent the teaching of socially dangerous ideas, (3) to promote cultural unity, (4) to provide criteria for choosing quality nonpublic schooling, and (5) to protect the public from dangerous business, health, and building practices.[34]

Essentially the courts have argued beginning with *Pierce* that the state can regulate private schools as long as they do not affect the viability of the organization.[35]

In *Wisconsin v. Yoder* the Supreme Court maintained that no matter how strong the State's interests in universal compulsory education, it could by no means enforce compulsory attendance to the exclusion of other considerations. In this case it was argued that in the balancing of state interests and parental religious beliefs, the beliefs of the parents and their First Amendment rights should be recognized and accommodated as much as possible.

The ultra-fundamentalists's legal argument against state regulation of Christian schools has been based primarily on the free exercise clause of the First Amendment. According to James Carper and Neal Devins:

The line distinguishing permissible from impermissible government conduct that infringes on religious freedom is not clearly drawn. This confusion results from a standard of review in which free exercise litigation is determining both the nature of the infringements on religious liberty and whether the state is using the least restrictive means available to it to further some compelling government interest.[36]

Lawsuits involving Christian schools in recent years have involved:

1. fire, health and safety,
2. curriculum,
3. textbook selection,
4. instructional time,
5. teacher certification,
6. zoning,
7. consumer protection,
8. student reporting,
9. state licensing,
10. community interaction, and
11. guidance requirements.[37]

In terms of these regulations, the most common source of conflict between Christian schools and the state has been over regulations controlling teaching practices, in particular curriculum, textbook and teacher certification.[38]

The contradictions at work in lower court decisions concerning the state regulation of Christian schools is perhaps nowhere as clear as in the case of teacher certification requirements. In *Kentucky State Board v. Rudasill*,[39] the Kentucky Supreme Court maintained that the state's certification requirements were unconstitutional. Graduation from a standard college or university, for example, was not seen as being absolutely essential to teach in a private school. In the case of the 1976 Ohio Supreme Court decision of *State vs. Whisner*,[40] the court maintained that the state's attempts to enforce teacher certification requirements were unconstitutional. As the court explained:

> In the face of the record before us, and in light of the expert testimony...it is difficult to imagine a state interest of sufficient magnitude to override the interest claiming protection under the free exercise clause. ...We will not, therefore, attempt to conjure up such an interest, in order to sustain application of the 'minimum standards' to these appellants.[41]

Contradictory opinions to those in Kentucky and Ohio were written in two decisions: *State vs. Faith Baptist Church*,[42] in which the Nebraska Supreme Court upheld a law requiring state teacher certification regulations and related statutes; and the North Dakota Supreme Court Case of *State vs. Shaver*,[43] which also upheld state teacher certification laws.

In the case of the Faith Baptist Church decision, the leadership of the school maintained that the state officials had no jurisdiction over "God's property." Everett Sileven and other church officials refused to:

1. provide a list of students enrolled in the school,
2. seek approval of the educational program,
3. employ certified teachers, and
4. seek general approval to operate the institution.[44]

The Faith Baptist Church case drew national attention. The issues raised by the case reflected the fundamental differences dividing state authorities and ultra-fundamentalists concerning the rights and prerogatives of the state versus those of individual citizens and religious groups. For technical reasons, as well as the extreme philosophical positoin taken by Sileven and the members of his congregation, Christian day school supporters urged that the case not be appealed to the Supreme Court.[45]

The issues of the regulation of Christian schools by state officials and prayer in the public schools are indicative of the complexity to be found in the controversies involving the ultra-fundamentalists and public education. In the case of school prayer, what is clearly at work is a conflict between cultures—over what our culture should be and what values it should support. For the ultra-fundamentalists, there is no inconsistency to be found in secterian religious belief being included in the program and curricular content of the public schools. This is despite the fact that the inclusion of such materials represents a violation of individual rights guaranteed by the Constitution. Ironically, it is the infringement of these rights that leads them to object to state interference with their schools. Seemingly, the ultra-fundamentalists will use the Constitution or support it in accord with whether or not it can be used to reinforce their particular religious position.

# Chapter Seven

# *Implications of the Ultra-Fundamentalist Critique of American Education*

Throughout American history the public schools have been the primary battleground for conflicts involving Church and State. With the resurgence since the late 1970s of religious fundamentalism as a social and political force at the national level, this battle has intensified and spread. According to James E. Wood, Jr., the Church-State conflicts have primarily been the result of "persistent and zealous efforts" intended to Christianize the public schools and eliminate the secular character guaranteed to them under the Constitution.[1]

The question arises as to why ultra-fundamentalist groups have focused so much of their attention on education and the public schools? In this concluding chapter, I will attempt to answer this question, as well as to develop some conclusions and personal reflections concerning the significance of the ultra-fundamentalists' battle to shape American public education.

## STATUS POLITICS AND CHRISTIAN FUNDAMENTALISM

The concept of status politics provides an important means by which to interpret the recent activities of ultra-fundamentalist groups in regards to education. Status politics is distinct from class politics. As Richard Pride and J. David Woodward have explained:

When individuals organize themselves into collectives which seek to use the power of government to protect or enhance their economic position or their claim to goods and services supplied by government, then they are engaged in *class* politics. When groups try to maintain or to increase the respect conferred on them by others, they are engaged in *status* politics. Class politics involves the clash over "bread and butter" interests; status politics involves confrontation over "lifestyles."[2]

Pride and Woodward establish the fact that "status politics is attitudinal rather than material."[3] In status politics symbolic benefits are sought, rather than material gains. Thus, the ultra-fundamentalists seek to have prayer included in the curriculum of the public schools, because it is a symbolic reaffirmation of their religious values and belief system. On the most basic level, nonbelievers would be compelled to recognize the status of those with ultra-fundamentalist religious beliefs.

In the case of the ultra-fundamentalists, status and recognition by the wider culture may be as much a social as a religious issue. The religious scholar Grant Wacker has argued that the increasing influence of Evangelical groups over the past two decades has not been so much a religious or theological movement, but instead one tied to "a cluster of values derived from Victorian middle-class society."[4] The emergence of fundamentalism as a more vocal movement in the 1970s and 1980s—a movement with "a particularly explicit set of social and cultural commit-ments"—is at least in part a response to the loss of power and status by a significant segment of American society.[5]

Implicit in this argument is the notion that although the Social Revolution of the 1960s empowered many individuals, it also diminished the influence and authority of those whose cultural and social values had predominated up until that time. Institutions such as mass media, public education and the Supreme Court clearly supported alternative visions of culture and society—ones that often conflicted with groups such as the ultra-fundamentalists. Social phenomenon such as the feminist movement and the "sexual revolution" challenged a culture that saw its roots in Norman Rockwell rather than in Jackson Pollock, that valued absolute rather than relative points of view, and a "Christian Civilization" rather than a Secular and Pluralistic society.

Tim LaHaye has argued that people like himself are engaged in "a battle for the mind," in which either man's wisdom (humanism) or God's wisdom (Christianity) will prevail. In fact, what is at play are competing value systems and the status and recognition afforded to individuals in the culture. On one level, the ultra-fundamentalists are fighting for a specific value system that is focused around their religious beliefs, and on another and closely related level, they are fighting for recognition and status as a cultural group.

The public educational system in the United States, with its diverse curriculum and relativistic point of view, threatens the ultra-fundamentalists' assumption that there are Absolute Truths and, ultimately, the status that they have held in American society. Controversies such as whether or not Creationism should be taught in the schools and whether or not prayer and Bible reading should be allowed, reflect a direct attempt on the part of the ultra-fundamentalists to gain equal status for their view of the world. In the end, cultural recognition, power and status are at the root of the conflict between the ultra-fundamentalists and the public education system in the United States.

The fact that the ultra-fundamentalists are seeking greater recognition in terms of their view of the world is neither unexpected, nor that different from the goals of other social or political groups in our country. The pursuit of status on the part of such groups has functioned historically as a driving force for groups as diverse as the Temperance Movement and the Suffrage Movement. During the 1960s, status was the primary issue pursued by woman and Blacks in the quest for greater Civil Rights. The more recent Gay Rights movement is essentially concerned with the same types of issues.

However, the ultra-fundamentalists do differ significantly from these other groups in a number of ways. First, their model of culture and society was dominant in the past. Their relative loss of status has occurred recently. In addition, they hold to an Absolute system of belief. In the closed religious system in which they function, there can be no compromise, no understanding and no common ground with those whom they believe are part of a secular world. Dialogue or compromise with individuals holding a different world-view is perceived by the ultra-fundamentalists as an incomplete rather than absolute commitment. In doing so, they see a refutation of the absolute belief or faith they hold.


## ULTRA-FUNDAMENTALISM AS A "TOTAL INSTITUTION"


In his valuable ethnographic study of a Fundamentalist Christian school entitled *God's Choice*, Alan Peshkin argues that Christian fundamentalist schools like the one he studied, represent a special type of "total institution."[6] Drawing on Erving Goffman's seminal essay "On the Characteristics of Total Institutions," Peshkin makes a convincing case that Christian schools not only have encompassing tendencies, but also tend to block interaction and discourse with groups that hold different values and ways of looking at the world.[7]

Peshkin's analysis encompasses a single school, which he refers to as Bethany Baptist Academy. While the students who attend the school do not eat and sleep there, he believes that its values totally direct their lives. When he asked a teacher: "What is the relationship between a teacher and student in your school?" Peshkin received this reply: "I feel closer to the kids because the Christian life is a total life. It's not just eight hours of school a day."[8]

Peshkin argues that:

> I believe BBA's leaders meant it to be a total institution, for a total institution is the natural organizational outcome of a school based on absolute truth. To be sure, total institutions are viewed variously as necessary but unpleasant places, as places to avoid, and, at their worst, as truly dreadful places. But Bethany's school is—in their terms—a benign total institution designed to serve the purposes of Christian parents and students.[9]

Bethany Baptist Academy is a closed system that protects its children from values and beliefs that do not conform to an ultra-fundamentalist perspective. It is a closed system—a "total institution"—based on an Absolute system of beliefs.

Peshkin explains that the purpose of Bethany Baptist Academy, together with the American Association of Christian Schools of which it is a member, is to:

1. bring children to salvation,
2. inform children about the Word of God,
3. keep children immersed in God,
4. keep children separate from the world,
5. encourage children to proselytize the unsaved,
6. to lead children into service as preachers, teachers and evangelists, and
7. failing the last point, have children become fully committed Christians, living their lives first and foremost for the glory of God.[10]

Such values are inconsistent with those found within the public school system in the United States. As an alternative school, Bethany Baptist Academy is not meant to develop highly informed citizens who can view domestic and world affairs from a series of different perspectives, nor to develop a pluralistic or multicultural perspective. Instead, it is intended to provide students with absolute values and a rigid point of view.

Peshkin's analysis of Bethany Baptist Academy can be extended to the ultra-fundamentalists in general. The ultra-fundamentalists have rooted their belief system in a series of absolutist dogmas based on their Christian faith. Their interpretation of "truth" totally pervades their lives and their understanding of the world. Everything that does not fit within their conception of knowledge is by definition an untruth or is false. Although they live within an open society, the ultra-fundamentalists wish to adopt a world view similar to that found within total institutions. The problem of course is that the great majority of the world does not subscribe to their belief system, and in fact sees such institutions as being highly threatening to human freedom and dignity.

In their battle for the control of the public schools, the ultra-fundamentalists are striving for status and recognition, as well as a desire to see their system of absolute truth recreated in the culture. By definition, they are missionaries whose purpose in life is to convert those who have not yet discovered Absolute Truth. As a result, it is impossible for them not to challenge the pluralistic model implicit in the public school system in the United States. Reaffirmation and confirmation of the secular is a contradiction of their belief in their Absolute vision of Christian Truth, and is therefore a profanation of their belief system.

## ON THE NATURE AND PURPOSE OF PUBLIC EDUCATION

The controversy over schooling raised by the ultra-fundamentalists ultimately focuses attention on a series of questions as to what is the nature and purpose of public education in the United States? Justice Felix Frankfurter argued in *McCollum v. Board of Education* that: "The public school is at once the symbol of our democracy and the most pervasive means of promoting our common destiny."[11] It is not surprising, therefore, that the public schools have become the major battleground in the conflict between the ultra-fundamentalists and the mainstream culture.

To a large degree it can be argued that the public schools are an embodiment of our law and more specifically the Constitution. Despite arguments made by ultra-fundamentalists to the contrary, the United States was founded as a secular state. It was the first nation to constitutionally prohibit the establishment of religion and also guarantee the free exercise of religion.[12] Significantly, the public school system as it developed during the nineteenth century has been avowedly secular. The foundation for its growth lies primarily in the work of Thomas Jefferson. In his "A Bill for the More General Diffusion of Knowledge," and in his *Notes on the State of Virginia*, Jefferson argued for the establishment of a system of public schools. Religious freedom was inseparably connected to his general program of public education. It was Jefferson's assumption as expressed in works such as his "Bill for Establishing Religious Freedom," that rational men needed education in order to arrive at religious truth, just as much as to achieve political wisdom; that basic education could be better obtained from state-sponsored schools than from state sponsored churches; and finally that the cause of religious truth could best be served by having all churches present their doctrines in a private rather than in a state context.[13] Jefferson's ideas were embodied by common school leaders such as Horace Mann. In his *Final Report to the Massachusetts State Board of Education*(1848) Mann wrote that:

> If a man is taxed to support a school where religious doctrines are inculcated which he believes to be false, and which he believes that God condemns, then he is excluded from the school by divine law, at the same time and he is compelled to support it by the human law. This is a double wrong.[14]

As a result of their belief in a single and absolute Christian truth, the ultra-fundamentalists do not feel, however, that the expression of their beliefs in the form of school prayer, Bible reading or the implementation of a Creationist curriculum, are inconsistent with the values of a democracy. Believing in absolutes, as do the ultra-fundamentalists, and living in a world where absolutist values prevail are two very different things. The United States is a heterogeneous culture. It is also a society based on democratic and secular political values. The demands made by the ultra-fundamentalists in the context of the public schools are ultimately inconsistent with the realities of American democracy.

The United States is not a theocracy based on Absolute Christian values. It is a democracy. It is a democracy that values toleration. Alan Peshkin argues in the conclusion to *God's Choice* that:

> The existence of fundamentalist Christian schools creates a paradox of pluralism in the United States. Paradoxes of pluralism testify to our ideological health. I hope the day never comes when our society feels that Christian schools must be suppressed in any way.[15]

Ironically, the pluralism that they find so offensive has played a critical role in the survival of the ultra-fundamentalists as a minority group within the culture.

Ultimately, the arguments of the ultra-fundamentalists are important, not because of the type of society they want to create, but because they remind us of the importance of toleration and the power of the Constitution. Peshkin cites the nineteenth century abolitionist Wendell Phillips to the effect that "External vigilance is the price of liberty."[16] Perhaps one of the great virtues of the recent debate concerning public education that has been raised by the ultra-fundamentalists is that they constantly remind us that in a democracy which has many different people with many different points of view, individual rights are not something that we can take for granted. We cannot afford to look:

> for an age when the people can be quiet and safe. At such times despotism, like a shrouding mist, steals over the mirror of freedom.[17]

## CONCLUSION

In conclusion, it is assumed among the ultra-fundamentalists that the United States is a Christian nation. While this may be so in terms of the country's historical tradition, and even though the majority of its people may be Christian, it is not Christian according to the law. On matters of religion, the Constitution is very clear. The United States is a secular state where all religions are tolerated and where no single religion, from a legal point of view, can ever dominate.

The public schools pose a threat to the ultra-fundamentalists because they operate under the assumption that a central feature "of political socialization is the cultivation and acceptance of diversity."[18] The ultra-fundamentalists, bound to a literal interpretation of the Bible, and a belief that the only truth is that revealed by their religion, are inevitably in conflict with the public schools and what they represent. By arguing that there is a single road to salvation and that there is only one way to worship the deity, tolerance of other religious groups, as well as other philosophies of life and politics becomes impossible for the ultra-fundamentalists.

The lack of tolerance found among the ultra-fundamentalists to other religious and social groups should not be taken lightly. Going beyond the issue of public education, they have developed a wide-ranging and comprehensive critique of contemporary American society. Topics as diverse as abortion, women's rights, states' rights and the control of media have become part of their agenda. Their impact has been undeniable. Yet, in the long run, their attack on public education may have more significance than all of these other areas combined. If public schooling is "a first corollary of democracy,"[19] then the ultra-fundamentalists' systematic attempts to undermine the public educational system in the United States represents a serious threat to the development of an informed and well-educated citizenry. The threat is a particularly subtle and invidious one, since in many respects it is being created by the very people who have historically been the mainstay of much of American society's values and traditions. It is also one that rejects science and many of the foundations of contemporary knowledge. As David Apter has argued in *Ideology and Discontent*:

> Today's American ideologue is a middle-class man who objects to his dependence on science even when he accepts its norms. He is resentful of the superiority of the educated and antagonistic to knowledge. His ideology is characteristically not of the left but of the right. It...looks back to a more bucolic age of individuality and localism, in which parochial qualities of mind were precisely those most esteemed—to a simple democracy, in fact...it is the ideology of all those who hitherto were the "staid" figures of our society in an earlier day; the models of once sober, industrious, and responsible citizens.[20]

Ultra-fundamentalist opposition to public education in the United States is rooted in a series of opposing religious and philosophical belief systems. Whereas for many individuals it is possible to reconcile a Christian faith with modern scientific theories, this is a task that is impossible for ultra-fundamentalists. As Henry Morris argues:

> there is no boundary or dichotomy between spiritual truth and secular truth; *all* things were created by God and are being sustained by Him.[21]

For Morris, and the ultra-fundamentalists in general, the possibility of a neutral or value free schooling is in fact impossible. Compromise with secular values cannot be tolerated, since compromise represents a rejection of transcendent values. Onalee McGraw explains:

> Value-free schooling is impossible because ultimately all educational endeavors must emanate from a world view that is either transcendent or humanistic. All concepts of the *meaning* of knowledge and of *what is worth knowing* must of necessity flow from religious and philosophical beliefs.[22]

Supporters of the public school system in the United States need to understand that reason and compromise are almost certainly not possible when dealing with the ultra-fundamentalists in matters concerning public education. Essentially, the most extreme elements of the fundamentalist movement in the United States have declared a war against the public schools.

The extent to which the image of warfare with the public schools is appropriate can be seen in many of the comments made by ultra-fundamentalists. Rousas J. Rushdoony, for example, argues that:

We are in the most important and crucial war of religion in all history, the struggle between Christianity and Humanism....It is a war unto death, and the goal of the battle is the obliteration of our faith. If this battle is nothing to you, the Lord may soon declare that you are nothing to Him.[23]

For Robert Allen Hill and Olaf John, the threat of secular values dominating the educational system is worse than the threat of communism:

The great threat to America today is not communist aggression, nuclear war or an oil embargo. The great threat is a public education system that has abandoned the principles upon which our nation was founded.[24]

Ultra-fundamentalists believe that they are engaged in nothing less than a holy war. In many instances, the imagery that they invoke is messianic— one that suggests the second coming of Christ:

Until Christ *does* return, therefore, we must do all we can both to reclaim our public schools and, even more importantly, in view of the time factor, to establish sound Christian schools, where every teacher is God called and properly prepared, and where all courses and textbooks completely conform to the principles of Scripture.[25]

Religious doctrine cannot, however, provide the basis for the development of a public policy in education. As Byrnes and Kiger have argued:

The rhetoric about harmonious relations between religion and democracy obscures an important contradiction; religious teachings imply a paradox. On the one hand, dominant religions in contemporary American society emphasize equality and justice. On the other hand, these religions embrace an exclusionary doctrine in which all individuals are considered unequal as aspirants for salvation. Some religious beliefs are distinctly not democratic since these beliefs imply that "only *certain* people are chosen people; that there is only one real truth—theirs."[26]

The ultra-fundamentalists, as well as certain other conservative religious groups, must be taken to task when they equate their values and beliefs as the only ones appropriate for American culture and society.

*Final Reflections*

This book has been written in an attempt to be as fair and objective as possible concerning the rights and needs of the ultra-fundamentalists. Many of their criticisms of American public education and our society are valid. Their concerns about State domination and control of public education and the protection of their civil and religious rights are reasonable. The ultra-fundamentalists' intolerance of other belief systems represents a prejudice and bigotry that is unacceptable in a democratic society such as the United States. Morality and religious doctrine simply cannot be equated in a democratic pluralistic culture. The ultra-fundamentalists are one of many groups protected by the First Amendment of the Constitution. In the pursuit of their rights, they do not have the right to impose their value system on others.

Up to this point, I have attempted to avoid presenting my personal and subjective feelings about the ultra-fundamentalists and their belief systems. I have attempted to make clear my own personal perspective and to recognize how that perspective has influenced the writing of this book. At this point, I wish to make several specific arguments and draw a seriers of conclusions based on what I believe is the role and function of public education in a democracy such as the United States.

To begin with, it is my belief that to accept the ultra-fundamentalists' arguments about public education is to accept an absolutist, intolerant and exclusive public school system. Such a public school system represents a conscious rejection of the pluralistic, tolerant and inclusive roots of American education.

As the poet American Walt Whitman wrote in his work *Leaves of Grass*: "We are a nation of nations and people of people." As a pluralistic culture of many nations, many people and many beliefs, we must respect the differences inherent in our plurality. In secular institutions such as the schools, specific religious beliefs cannot play a role, not because they are not important in our private lives, but because our diversity and commitment to personal freedom as a democratic culture makes their inclusion impossible.

The greatest lesson to be drawn from the ultra-fundamentalists is that they provide a mirror for our democracy—one that can provide the basis for a dialogue concerning the nature and purpose of education in a pluralistic culture. In a sense, the ultra-fundamentalist controversy over the public schools provides us with an instrument with which to measure the degree to which the schools are supportive of pluralistic, tolerant and inclusive principles.

Examples of this process can be seen in a number of instances discussed in this book. What values, for example, are expressed in mass circulated textbooks? Are they reflective of a whole spectrum, or do they focus on a limited range of concepts and ideologies? The ultra-fundamentalists have a valid point when they argue that current social studies and history textbooks tend to deemphasize the role that religion has played in the history of our country.

Yet while maintaining that the mainstream culture does not have the right to exclude the ultra-fundamentalists' point of view from the content of textbooks, they do not have the right to stubbornly maintain an absolutist point of view that precludes the rights of those whose views differ from their own.

The ultra-fundamentalists have the right to demand that alternative models of education be tolerated. Christian schools have every right to exist. The mainstream culture must, and in point of fact largely does, support such alternatives.

Yet in maintaining the right of alternative schools to exist, the mainstream culture and its agent, the state, has the right and obligation to see that minimal standards are maintained. These involve not only health and physical standards, but curricular content where appropriate. Thus the state has the right to demand that students are provided with basic instruction in those fields necessary for them to become useful and productive citizens. If such a position is implemented with reasonable sensitivity to and in collaboration with the groups involved in alternative educational programs, it should not, in most instances, interfere with the philosophical belief systems of the alternative groups.

Finally, if they indeed support an inclusive and pluralistic model of education and culture, then the public schools should not deal with the ultra-fundamentalists as a threat to public education, but simply as another special interest group in the culture. Accommodation, compromise and empathy are essential to both sides. In dealing with the ultra-fundamentalist perspective we must avoid the ultra-fundamentalist pitfall of being absolutist, intolerant and exclusive.

Such a view recognizes much more clearly than the public educational system has been willing to admit that education is neither neutral nor value free. A pluralistic culture such as the United States represents a range of different, and at times conflicting points of view.

The ultra-fundamentalists must in the end honestly decide what their relationship to public education is going to be. They attempt to function with majority status, when in fact they are not a majority. They rightly demand tolerance and alternatives, when in fact they try to reject them for others. Such positions are not only inconsistent with democratic principles, but with the historical evolution of the American educational system.

The ultra-fundamentalists have the right to promote their beliefs and to maintain their rights, but not to impose their vision of culture and education on the majority of the American schoolchildren. American public education is not, and cannot function as a total institution that subscribes to a fundamentalist—or for that matter any other exclusive ideology.

# Notes

## INTRODUCTION

1. For the purposes of this study the following definitions are used: (1) the term Evangelical refers to American Protestants who stress conservative doctrines and morality, together with a traditional or literal interpretation of the Bible. An individual commitment to Jesus Christ and missionizing is an important part of their belief system. (2) Fundamentalist refers to militant Evangelicals who hold to the inerrency of the Scriptures. They keep their churches strictly separate from Christians with different religious points of view, including moderate Evangelicals.

My use of the term ultra-fundamentalism is based on the work of David Bollier. In his book *Liberty and Justice for Some: Defending a Free Society from the Radical Right's Holy War on Democracy* (Washington, D.C.: People for the American Way, 1982), p. 3, Bollier argues that:

> The current vocabulary used to describe the political agenda of Jerry Falwell, Phyllis Schafly, and their colleagues is inadequate. The term "new Right" does not properly apply to these leaders and their groups because the New Right is a separate, distinct—and more secular—brand of politics (even though the two cooperate extensively). The term "fundamentalist" is likewise misleading because many fundamentalist Christians abhor the political values of Falwell and his friends. Similarly, to call these activists "conservatives" is inaccurate, and distasteful to *bona fide* conservatives.

In order to clear up this linguistic confusion, Bollier coins the phrases "ultra-fundamentalism" and "moral majoritarian." The term "ultra-fundamentalist" is, in the author's opinion, the most useful and the one that will be used throughout this work. It is used to describe a group of:

> activists whose political views are intertwined with a certain brand of religious belief and expressed by groups like Moral Majority, Inc., the

Christian Voice, the National Christian Action Coalition, and the Religious Roundtable. *Ibid.*

2. Tim LaHaye, *The Battle for the Mind* (Old Tappan, New Jersey: Fleming H. Revell Company, 1980), p. 26.

3. Kenneth Woodward with Eloise Saholz, "The Right's New Bogeyman," *Newsweek*, 6 July, 1981, p. 48.

4. Francis A. Schaeffer, *How Should We Then Live: The Rise and Decline of Western Culture and Thought* (Old Tappan, New Jersey: Fleming H. Revell Company, 1976), p. 226.

5. Homer Duncan, *Secular Humanism*, (Lubbock, Texas: Missionary Crusader, 1980), p. 4.

6. LaHaye, *The Battle for the Mind*, p. 36.

7. *Ibid.*, p. 39.

8. *Ibid.*

9. *Ibid.*, p. 19.

10. The *Humanist Manifesto, I*, was originally written in 1933 and updated by leading writers and thinkers such as Sidney Hook, B. F. Skinner and Isaac Asimov in 1973. See: *Humanist Manifestos, I and II* (New York: Prometheus Books, 1973).

11. Duncan, *Secular Humanism*, p. 30.

12. *Ibid.*

13. *Ibid.*, p. 7.

14. Quoted by Duncan, *Ibid*, p. 42.

15. Francis A. Schaeffer, *A Christian Manifesto* (Westchester, Illinois: Crossway Books, 1981), pp. 54-55. Similar arguments are made by other ultra-fundamentalist writers. According to John W. Whitehead and John Conlan in a 1978 article for the *Texas Tech Law Review*, secular humanism received official recognition as a religion when the Supreme Court decided that nontheists could register as conscientious objectors. According to their argument:

> Secularism is nontheistic and "humanism" is secular because it excludes the basic tenets of theism. Therefore, secular humanism is nontheistic. However, while secular humanism is nontheistic, it is religious because it directs itself towards religious beliefs and practices that are in active opposition to traditional theism. Humanism is a doctrine centered solely on human interests and values. Therefore, humanism defies Man Collectively and individually, whereas Theism worships God.

Following the logic of Whitehead and Conlan's argument, Communism, Atheism and Agnosticism all have to be considered religions since they are "in active opposition to traditional theism." See: John W. Whitehead and John Conlan, "The Establishment of the Religion of Secular Humanism and Its First Amendment Implications," *Texas Tech Law Review*, vol. 10, no. 1, 1979, p. 29.

16. *Ibid*, p. 55. It is worth noting that a widely recognized religion such as Buddhism can be reasonably subsumed within this definition.

17. *Ibid*, p. 53.

18. *Ibid*, pp. 57-58.

19. *The American Heritage Dictionary of the English Language*, William Morris, ed. (New York: Houghton Mifflin Co., 1973), p. 1099.

20. Tim LaHaye, *The Battle for the Mind*, p. 43.

21. Quoted from Mel and Norma Gabler's *Handbook No. 1* by David Bolliner, *Liberty and Justice for Some*, p. 132.

22. Jerry Falwell, *America Can be Saved* (Murfreesboro, TN.: Sword of the Lord Publishers, 1979), p. 53.

23. Quoted by Bollier, *Liberty and Justice for Some*, p. 135. "700 Club" broadcast, October 2, 1981.

24. Julius Lester, "Morality and Education," *Democracy*, April 1982, pp. 28-29.

25. Onalee McGraw, *Secular Humanism and the Schools: The Issue Whose Time Has Come* (Washington, D.C.: The Heritage Foundation, 1976), p. 5.

26. Diane Ravitch, "The New Right and the Schools," *American Educator*, vol. 6, no. 3, (Fall 1982) p. 13.

## CHAPTER 1

1. United States District Court Eastern District of Arkansas Western Division, William R. Overton, United States District Judge, *Rev. Bill McLean v. the Arkansas Board of Education et al.*, January 5, 1982, p. 3.

2. George M. Marsden, *Fundamentalism and American Culture, the Shaping of Twentieth-Century Evangelicalism: 1870-1925* (New York: Oxford University Press, 1980), p. 3. For background on fundamentalism in American culture see in addition to Marsden: Stewart G. Cole, *The History of Fundamentalism* (Hamden, CT: Archon Books, 1963); Ernest R. Sandeen, *The Roots of Fundamentalism: British and American Millenerianism, 1800-1930* (Chicago: The

University of Chicago Press, 1970); Charles Allyn Russell, *Voices of American Fundamentalism: Seven Biographical Studies* (Philadelphia: The Westminster Press, 1976); and James Barr, *Fundamentalism* (Philadelphia: The Westminster Press, 1978).

3. Marsden, *Fundamentalism and American Culture*, p. 3.

4. *Ibid.*

5. For background on the Scopes trial see *Marsden*, pp. 184-188; and Edward J. Larson, "Outlawing Evolution, 1920-1925." Chapter 2 in *Trial and Error: The American Controversy Over Creation and Evolution* (New York: Oxford University Press, 1985), pp. 28-57.

6. Marsden, *Fundamentalism and American Culture*, pp. 185-86.

7. *Ibid*, p. 199.

8. Richard Hofstader, *Anti-Intellectualism in American Life* (New York: 1962), p. 121.

9. William McLoughlin, "Is there a Third Force in Christendom?", *Dadelus*, Vol. 46, (Winter 1967) pp. 43-68.

10. Sandeen, *The Roots of Fundamentalism, op. cit.*

11. LaHaye, *The Battle for the Mind*, p. 182.

12. *Ibid.*

13. Marsden, *Fundamentalism and American Culture*, p. 228.

14. See Barr, "What is Fundamentalism?" Chap. 1 in *Fundamentalism*, pp. 1-10 for a detailed overview of the complexities defining fundamentalism as a personal, social and religious movement.

15. John Dewey, *Democracy and Education: An Introduction to the Philosophy of Education* (New York: The Free Press, 1966).

16. Rousas J. Rushdoony, *The Messianic Character of American Education: Studies in the History of the Philosophy of Education* (Nutley, N.J.: The Craig Press, 1972).

17. Rousas J. Rushdoony, *Intellectual Schizophrenia: Culture, Crisis and Education* (Philadelphia: The Presbyterian and Reformed Publishing Company, 1973).

18. *Ibid*, p. 10.

20. *Ibid.*

21. *Ibid*, pp. 10-11.

22. *Ibid*, p. 11.

23. *Ibid*, p. 10.

24. *Ibid*, p. 19.

25. Introduction by Rushdoony to Alan N. Grover's *Ohio's Trojan Horse: A Warning to Christian Schools Everywhere* (Greenville, S.C.: Bob Jones University Press, Inc., 1977), p. 31.

26. Rushdoony, *The Messianic Character of American Education*, p. 31.

27. *Ibid*.

28. *Ibid*, p. 323.

29. *Ibid*, p. 144.

30. *Ibid*, p. 145.

31. *Ibid*, pp. 145-147.

32. Barbara Morris, *Change Agents in the Schools* (Upland, Calif.: The Barbara M. Morris Report, 1979).

33. Barbara Morris writing in *The National Educator*, July 1977, p. 1.

34. Quoted by Charlges J. Park, "Preachers, Politics, and Public Education: A Review of Right-Wing Pressures Against Public Schooling in America," *Phi Delta Kappan*, May 1980, p. 611.

35. Barbara M. Morris, "The Real Issue in Education as Seen by a Journalist on the Far Right," *Phi Delta Kappan*, May 1980, p. 613.

36. LaHaye, *The Battle for the Mind*, p. 43.

37. Henry Morris, *Education for the Real World* (San Diego: Creation Life Publishers, 1977), pp. 22-23.

38. LaHaye, *The Battle for the Mind*, p. 44.

39. For a detailed, and at the same time, highly critical review and bibliography of the Revisionists see: Diane Ravitch, "The Revisionists Revised: Studies in the Historiography of American Education," *Proceedings of the National Academy of Education,* vol. 4, 1977, pp. 1-84. Ravitch's study was later expanded and published as *The Revisionists Revised: A Critique of the Radical Attack on Schools* (New York: Basic Books, 1978). A response by the Revisionists to Ravitch's critique is included in Walter Feiberg, Harvey Kantor, Michael Katz and Paul Violas's *Revisionists Respond to Ravitch* (Washington, D.C.: National Academy of Education, 1980).

## CHAPTER 2

1. Stephen Arons, *Compelling Belief: The Culture of American Schooling* (New York: McGraw-Hill Book Company, 1983), p. 16.

2.. *Ibid.*

3. Onalee McGraw, *Family Choice in Education: The New Imperative* (Washington, D.C.: The Heritage Foundation, 1978), p. 2.

4. *Ibid*, p. 20.

5. *Ibid*, p. 21.

6. See, for example, Edward B. Jenkinson, *Censors in the Classroom: The Mind Benders* (Carbondale, IL: Southern Illinois Press, 1979); and Edward B. Jenkinson, *The Schoolbook Protest Movement: 40 Questions and Answers* (Bloomington, IN: Phi Delta Kappa, 1986).

7. Jenkinson, *Censors in the Classroom*, p. xii.

8. Ethel Herr, *Schools: How Parents Can Make a Difference* (Chicago: Moody Press, 1981), pp. 204-205.

10. Connaught Marshner, *Blackboard Tyranny* (New Rochelle, N.Y.: Arlington House, 1978), p. 242.

11. *Ibid*, p. 246.

12. Mel and Norma Gabler, "A Parent's Guide to Textbook Review and Reform," Special Supplement to *Education Update*, (Winter, 1978), pp. 2-3.

13. *Ibid*, p. 3.

14. *Ibid.*

15. Jenkinson, *Censors on the Classroom*, p. 83. The text of the Hatch Amendment is as follows:

PROTECTION OF PUPIL RIGHTS

Sec. 1250. Section 439 of the General Education Provisions Act (relating to the protection of pupil rights) is amended by inserting...a new subsection as follows:

**(b) No student shall be required, as part of any applicable program to submit to psychiatric examination, testing, or treatment, or psychological examination, testing, or treatment, in which the primary purpose is to reveal information concerning:

"(1) political affiliations;

"(2) mental and psychological problems potentially embarrassing to the student or his family;

"(3) sex behavior and attitudes;

"(4) illegal, anti-social, self-incriminating and demeaning behavior;

"(5) critical appraisals of other individuals with whom respondents have close family relationships;

"(6) legally recognized privileged and analogous relationships, such as those of lawyers, physicians, and ministers; or

"(7) income (other than required by law to determine eligibility for participation in a program receiving financial assistance under such program), without the prior consent of the student (if the student is an adult or emancipated minor), or in the case of unemancipated minor, without the prior written consent of the parent." Reproduced in Barbara Parker and Stefanie Weiss, *Protecting the Freedom to Learn: A Citizen's Guide* (Washington, D.C.: People for the American Way, 1983), p. 80.

16. *Ibid*, p. 8.

17. *Ibid*, p. 83.

18. Quoted by Jenkinson, *Censors in the Classroom*, p. 85.

19. *Ibid*.

20. Onalee McGraw, "Who is Censoring Books? The Debate Continues," *Education Update*. vol. 6, no. 4, (October 1982), p. 1.

21. *Ibid*. A convincing case for the ultra-fundamentalists' point of view is presented by Paul C. Vitz in his book *Censorship: Evidence of Bias in Our Children's Textbooks* (Ann Arbor, MI: Servant Books, 1986).

22. Parker and Weiss, *Protecting the Freedom to Learn*, p. 11.

23. People for the American Way, *Attacks on Freedom to Learn: A 1984-1985 Report* (Washington, D.C.: People for the American Way, 1986), p. 1.

24. *Ibid*.

25. Parker and Weiss, *Protecting the Freedom to Learn*, p. 10.

26. People for the American Way, *Attacks on Freedom to Learn*, p. 2.

27. *Ibid*, p. 15.

28. *Ibid*, p. 13.

29. *Ibid*, p. 22.

30. *Ibid*, p. 15.

31. *Ibid*, p. 22.

32. *Ibid*, p. 2.

33. John Egerton, "The Battle for the Books," *The Progressive*, 1976, vol. 39, no. 6, p. 13.

34. James C. Hefley, *Are Textbooks Harming Your Children? Norma and Mel Gabler Take Action and Show You How!* (Milford, MI: Mott Media, 1979), p. 160.

35. Jenkinson, *Censors in the Classroom*, p. 18.

36. Hefley, *Are Textbooks Harming*, p. 157.

37. *Ibid*, p. 19.

38. Jenkinson, *Censors in the Classroom*, p. 20.

39. *Ibid*.

40. Franklin Parker, *The Battle of the Books: Kanawha County* (Bloomington, IN: Phi Delta Kappa, 1975), p. 13.

41. *Ibid*, p. 21.

42. Hefley, *Are Textbooks Harming*, p. 158.

43. *Ibid*, p. 176.

44. *Jenkinson*, p. 22.

45. *Ibid*, pp. 22-23.

46. Hefley, *Are Textbooks Harming*, p. 167.

47. Robert O'Neil, *Classrooms in the Crossfire: The Rights and Interests of Students, Parents, Teachers, Administrators, Librarians and the Community* (Bloomington, IN: Indiana University Press, 1981), pp. 6-7.

48. Jenkinson, *Censors in the Classroom*, p. 27.

49. *Ibid*, pp. 23-24.

50. *Ibid*, p. 26.

51. Quoted by Jenkinson, *Censors in the Classroom*, p. 26.

52. *Ibid*, p. 27.

53. *Arons*, p. 5.

54. *Ibid*, p. 6.

55. *Ibid*, p. 8.

56. *Ibid*, p. 12.

57. *Ibid*, p. 9.

58. Colin Campbell, "Book Banning in America," *New York Times Book Review*, 20 December 1981, p. 1.

59. Joseph Nocera, "The Big Book Banning Brawl," *The New Republic*, 13 September 1982, p. 24.

60. *Ibid*, p. 24.

61. *Ibid*, p. 24.

62. William R. Ball, "Opting Out of Reading Class in Tennessee: The Only Possible Outcome," *Education Week*, 3 December 1986, p. 24.

63. *Ibid*, p. 19.

64. Quoted by Jenkinson, *The School Protest Movement*, p. 20.

65. *Ibid*, p. 20.

66. *Ibid*, pp. 20-21.

67. Phyllis Schafly, "Fact and Fiction About Censorship," (Washington, D.C.: National Defense Committee, National Society, Daughters of the American Revolution, 1984), p. 1.

68. Jenkinson, *The Schoolbook Protest Movement*, p. 7.

## CHAPTER 3

1. Throughout American history the content of textbooks has been an important source of controversy and debate. Immediately following the American Revolution, for example, a conscious effort was made by American authors such as Noah Webster to write textbook materials that reflected a specifically American rather than British value system. In the decades immediately preceding the Civil War, Southern writers and educators objected to the ideological content (pro-abolitionist) of textbook materials written and published in the Northern states and used in the South. In much the same way, and for many of the same reasons, Catholic educators started to publish their own textbooks in the middle of the nineteenth century—ones reflecting their own specific values and belief systems rather than those of the mainstream or general culture. For historical background on the role that textbooks have played in American culture see: Ruth Miller Elson's, *Guardians of Tradition: American Schoolbooks in the Nineteenth Century* (Lincoln, Nebraska: University of Nebraska Press, 1964); and John Nietz, *Old Textbooks* (Pittsburgh: University of Pittsburgh Press, 1961).

2. Edward B. Jenkinson, *Censors in the Classroom: The Mind Benders* (Carbondale, IL: Southern Illinois University Press, 1979), p. xv.

3. The best general source for background material on the Gablers is provided by James C. Hefley's, *Are Textbooks Harming Your Children? Norma and Mel Gabler Take Action and Show You How!* (Milford, MI: Mott Media, 1979). Also see: Ann Weissmann, "Building the Tower of BABEL," *Texas Outlook*, vol. 65, no. 4, (Winter 1981-82); and Rita Ciolli, "The Politics of Textbooks," *APF Reporter*, vol. 7, no. 1, (Winter 1982).

4. Hefley, *Are Textbooks Harming*, p. 15.

5. *Ibid*, p. 15.

6. William Martin, "The Guardians Who Slumbereth Not," *Texas Monthly*, (November, 1982), p. 145.

7. *Ibid*, p. 146.

8. Hefley, *Are Textbooks Harming*, p. 20.

9. *Ibid*, p. 42.

10. *Ibid*, p. 49.

11. Martin, "Guardians," p. 146.

12. Barbara Parker, "Your Schools May be the Next Battlefield in the Crusade Against 'Improper' Textbooks," *The American School Board Journal*, (June 1979), p. 21.

13. Martin, "Guardians," p. 146.

14. Mel and Norma Gabler, "Humanism in Textbooks (Secular Religion in the Classroom)," The Mel Gablers, P.O. Box 7518, Longview, Texas (1983).

15. *Ibid*, p. 2.

16. *Ibid*.

17. *Ibid*.

18. *Ibid*.

19. *Ibid*, p. 4.

20. *Ibid*.

21. *Ibid*.

22. *Ibid*.

23. Martin, "Guardians," p. 150.

24. The MacNeil-Lehrer Report, "The Texas Textbook Debate," 10 November 1982, p. 1.

25. Norma and Mel Gabler, "A Parent's Guide to Textbook Review and Reform." (Washington, D.C.: The Heritage Foundation, 1978).

26. *Ibid*, p. 2.

27. *Ibid*.

28. Parker, "Your Schools," p. 21.

29. Hefley, *Are Textbooks Harming*, p. 202.

30. Edward B. Jenkinson, *The Schoolbook Protest Movement* (Bloomington, Indiana: Phi Delta Kappa Educational Foundation, 1986), p. 7.

31. Jerry Falwell, "Textbooks in Public Schools: A Disgrace and Concern to America," *Journal Champion*, 4 May 1979, p. 1, quoted by Jenkinson. *Censors in the Classroom*, (Schoolbook Protest Movement) p. 67.

32. *Ibid*.

33. Tim LaHaye, *The Battle for the Public Schools* (Old Tappan, N.J.: Fleming H. Revel, 1983), p. 193.

34. *Ibid*, p. 80.

35. Onalee McGraw, *Secular Humanism and the Schools: The Issue Whose Time Has Come* (Washington, D.C.: The Heritage Foundation, 1976), p. 4.

36. *Ibid*.

37. Louis E. Raths, Merrill Harmin and Sidney B. Simon, *Values and Teaching* (Columbus, OH: Charles E. Merrill Publishing Co., 1966), p. 28. Probably the single-most widely circulated work in the field of Values Clarification is by Sidney B. Simon, Leland W. Howe, and Howard Kirschenbaum, *Values Clarification: A Handbook of Practical Strategies for Teachers and Students* (New York: Hart Publishing Company, 1972).

38. Tim LaHaye, *The Battle for the Public Schools* (Old Tappan, N.J.: Fleming H. Revell Company, 1983), p. 173.

39. Onalee McGraw, *Secular Humanism*, p. 6.

40. *Ibid*.

41. *Ibid*.

42. Onalee McGraw, *Family Choice in Education: The New Imperative* (Washington, D.C.: The Heritage Foundation, 1978), p. 16. This summary of Kohlberg is taken directly from McGraw.

43. *Ibid*, p. 18.

44. *Ibid*, p. 19.

45. *Ibid*, p. 20.

46. LaHaye, *Battle*, p. 175.

47. *Ibid*, p. 178.

48. Dorothy Nelkin, *The Creation Controversy: Science or Scripture in the Schools* (New York: W.W. Norton & Company, 1982), p. 48.

49. *Ibid*, p. 49.

50. Quoted by Nelkin, *ibid*, p. 50.

51. *Ibid*, pp. 51-52.

52. *Ibid*, p. 51.

53. *Ibid.*

54. *Ibid*, p. 125.

55. "MACOS—Study in Adultery, Suicide and Murder," *Sex Education and Mental Health Report*, 10 (Winter 1980), quoted by LaHaye, *Battle*, pp. 193-195.

56. *Ibid*, pp. 194-195.

57. *Ibid.*

58. *Ibid*, p. 196.

59. *Ibid.*

60. *Ibid*, p. 203.

61. *Ibid*, p. 204.

62. *Ibid.*

63. *Ibid*, p. 204.

64. *Ibid.*

65. Gablers, "Humanism in Textbooks," p. 6.

66. *Ibid*, quoted by the Gablers.

67. *Ibid.*

68. *Ibid.*

69. *Ibid.*

70. Barbara Morris, *Change Agents in the Schools* (Upland, Calif.: The Barbara M. Morris Report, 1979), p. 176.

71. *Ibid*, p. 177.

72. LeHaye, *Battle*, p. 214-225.

73. *Ibid*, p. 222.

74. *Ibid*, p. 225.

75. *Ibid*, p. 182.

76. *Ibid*.

77. Morris, *Change Agents*, p. 15.

78. *Ibid*.

79. *Ibid*, p. 17.

80. *Ibid*.

81. Henry M. Morris, *Education for the Real World* (San Diego: Creation Life Publishers, 1978), p. 28.

## CHAPTER 4

1. Dorothy Nelkin, *The Creation Controversy: Science or Scripture in the Schools* (New York: W.W. Norton & Company, 1982), p. 25.

2. Waynes A. Moyer, *Scopes Revisited: Evolution v. Biblical Creationism* (Washington, D.C.: People for the American Way, 1983), p. 1.

3. Henry M. Morris, *Education for the Real World* (San Diego: Creation Life Publishers, 1978), p. 48.

4. Quoted by Nelkin, *Creation Controversy*, p. 32.

5. *Ibid*, p. 33.

6. *Ibid*, p. 138.

7. Quoted by Edward J. Larson, *Trial and Error: The American Controversy Over Creation and Evolution* (New York: Oxford University Press, 1985), p. 101.

8. Kern Alexander, *School Law* (St. Paul, Minn.: West Publishing Company, 1980), p. 302-303.

9. *Ibid*, p. 303.

10. *Ibid.*

11. *Ibid*, p. 292.

12. *Ibid*, p. 120.

13. Larson, *Trial and Error*, p. 122.

14. Max Rafferty, Superintendent of Public Instruction, *Guidelines for Moral Instruction in California: A Report Accepted by the State Board of Education*, (Sacramento: California State Department of Education, 9 May, 1969).

15. John A. Moore, "Creation in California," *Dadelus*, p. 177.

16. *Science Framework for California Public Schools. Kindergarten— Grades One Through Twelve.* Prepared by the California State Advisory Committee on Science Education and adopted by the California State Board of Education (Sacramento: California State Department of Education, 1969).

17. Moore, "Creation", p. 177.

18. *Ibid*, p. 178.

19. The Creation Research Society was set up in 1963 by the horticulturist Dr. Walter E. Lammert. Morris, an hydraulics engineer by training, served as the president of the organization for six years after Lammert. The Society has 400 voting members and 1,200 associate members. *Ibid*, p. 188.

20. For a description of Christian Heritage College's operation see: Frank Viviano, "The Crucifixion of Evolution: What Your Kids Will be Learning this Fall," *Mother Jones*, Sept./Oct., 1981, pp. 22, 24-26, 30, 56-59.

21. *Ibid*, p. 26.

22. Henry M. Morris, "Evolution, Creation and the Public Schools," *Creation: Acts, Facts and Impacts*, ed. Henry M. Morris, Duane T. Gish and George M. Hillestad (San Diego, California: Creation Life Publishers, 1974), p. 109.

23. Henry M. Morris, *Education for the Real World* (San Diego: Creation Life Publishers, 1978), p. 50.

24. Morris, "Evolution", p. 109.

25. Morris, *Education for the Real World*, p. 77.

26. *Ibid*, p. 61.

27. Quoted by LaHaye, *Battle for the Mind*, p. 64.

28. *Ibid*, p. 61.

29. Morris, "Evolution," p. 109.

30. Morris, *Education for the Real World*, p. 7.

31. Morris, "Evolution," p. 110. According to Morris: "Humanism and all other anti-Christian philosophies are based squarely on the assumption of evolution, and it has been clearly shown by creationist scientists that special creation is a much better scientific explanation for the world than evolution." Henry M. Morris, *Education for the Real World*, p. 8.

32. Duane Gish, "Creation-Evolution," *Creation: Acts, Facts and Impacts*, ed. Henry M. Morris, Duane T. Gish and George M. Hillestad (San Diego, California: Creation Life Publishers, 1974), p. 138.

33. Wendell Bird, "Freedom of Religion and Science Instruction in Public Schools," *Yale Law Journal*, vol. 83 (1978), pp. 516-17, nn. 8-9.

34. Larson, *Trial and Error*, p. 148.

35. *Ibid.*

36. *Ibid*, p. 150.

37. *Ibid*, p. 151.

38. For a detailed background of the case see Nelkin, "Legislating Science in Arkansas." Chap. 9; *Creation Controversy*, pp. 137-147, and Appendix 1, pp. 199-228.

39. *Ibid*, p. 228.

40. *Ibid.*

41. Thomas J. Flygare, "The Case of Segraves v. State of California," *Phi Delta Kappan*, vol. 63, no. 2 (October 1981), pp. 98-99.

42. Quoted by Flygare, *Ibid*, p. 99.

43. *Ibid*, p. 99.

44. Larson, *Trial and Error*, p. 164.

45. Murray Gell-Mann, "First Word," *Omni*, vol. 9, no. 5 (February 1987), p. 8.

46. *Ibid.*

47. *Ibid.*

48. *Ibid.*

49. *Ibid.*

50. Harvey Siegel, "Creationism, Evolution, and Education: The California Fiasco," *Phi Delta Kappan*, vol. 63, no. 2, p. 99.

51. *Ibid*, p. 100.

52. *Ibid*.

53. *Ibid*.

54. Supreme Court of the United States, *Edwards, Governor of Louisiana, et al. v. Aquillard et al.*, No. 85-1513. Argued December 10, 1986-Decided June 19, 1987. This case is reproduced in West's *Education Law Reporter*, vol. 39, no. 3 (August 1987), pp. 2573-2607.

55. *Ibid*, p. i.

56. *Ibid*, p. ii.

57. *Ibid*.

58. *Ibid*.

59. *Ibid*.

60. Larson, *Trial and Error*, p. 170.

## CHAPTER 5

1. David Bollier, *Liberty and Justice for Some: Defending a Free Society from the Radical Holy War on Democracy* (Washington, D.C.: People for the American Way, 1982), p. 218.

2. Onalee McGraw, *Family Choice in Education: The New Imperative* (Washington, D.C.: The Heritage Foundation, 1978), p. 24.

3. *Ibid*, p. 2.

4. *Ibid*, p. 1.

5. *Ibid*.

6. Tim LaHaye, *Battle for the Mind* (Old Tappen, N.J.: Fleming H. Revel Company, 1980), p. 211.

7. Barbara Morris, *Change Agents in the Schools* (Upland, Calif.: The Barbara Morris Report, 197?), p. 64.

8. *Ibid*, p. 65.

9. *Ibid*, p. 67.

10. *Ibid*, p. 68.

11. *Ibid*, p. 70.

12. *Ibid*, p. 71.

13. *Pierce v. Society of the Sisters of the Holy Names of Jesus and Mary.* Supreme Court of the United States, 268 U.S. 510, 45 S.Ct 571 (1925).

14. Kern Alexander, *School Law* (St. Paul, Minn.: West Publishing Co., 1980), p. 272.

15. *Ibid*, p. 256.

16. *Ibid*, p. 274.

17. Onalee McGraw, *Family Choice in Education*, p. 28; citing Stephen Arons, "The Separation of School and State: *Pierce* Reconsidered," *Harvard Educational Review*, vol. 46, no. 1, (February 1976), pp. 80-104.

18. Morris, *Change Agents*, p. 143.

19. LaHaye, *The Battle for the Public Schools*, p. 153.

20. Cited by Morris, *Change Agents*, p. 34.

21. Alexander, p. 278.

22. LaHaye, *The Battle for the Mind*, p. 197.

23. Quoted by Bollier, *Liberty and Justice*, p. 239.

24. *Ibid*, p. 239.

25. *The Fundamentalist Phenomenon: The Resurgence of Conservative Christianity*, eds. Jerry Falwell with Ed Dobson and Ed Hindson (Garden City, N.Y.: Doubleday-Galilee Original, 1981), p. 203.

26. *Ibid*, pp. 203-204.

27. *Ibid*, p. 206.

28. John E. Coons and Stephen D. Sugarman, *Education by Choice: The Case for Family Control* (Berkeley, Calif.: University of California Press, 1978).

29. *Ibid*, p. xi.

30. *Ibid*, p. 1.

31. *Ibid*.

32. *Ibid*.

## CHAPTER 6

1. Quoted from the *Family Protection Report, June 1980* by David Bollier, *Liberty and Justice for Some: Defending a Free Society from the Radical Holy War on Democracy* (Washington, D.C.: People for the American Way, 1982), p. 208.

2. *Ibid*, p. 205.

3. LaHaye, *Battle for the Mind*, p. 167.

4. Quoted by Kern Alexander, *School Law* (St. Paul, Minn.: West Publishing Company, 1980), p. 166.

5. *Ibid*, pp. 166-167.

6. *Everson v. Board of Education*, Supreme Court of the United States, 330 U.S. 1, 67 S.Ct. 504 (1947).

7. *Ibid*, p. 184.

8. *Engle v. Vitale*, 370 U.S. 421, 82, S.Ct. 1261 (1962).

9. *Ibid*, pp. 239-240.

10. *School District of Abington Township v. Schempp and Murray v. Curlett*, Supreme Court of the United States, 374 U.S. 203, 83 SCt. 1560 (1963).

11. *Ibid*, p. 246.

12. *Ibid*.

13. Lou Cannon, "Hill Gets Reagan's Prayer Amendment," *The Washington Post*, 18 May 1982.

14. Quoted by Bollier, *Liberty and Justice*, p. 203.

15. R. Freeman Butts, *Religion, Education and the First Amendment: The Appeal to History* (Washington, D.C.: People for the American Way, 1986), pp. 6-7.

16. George F. Will, *Newsweek*, 7 June 1982.

17. James J. Kilpatrick, *The Washington Post*, 10 December 1981, quoted by David Bollier, *Liberty and Justice*, p. 211.

18. Phyllis Schlafly, "Alabama Parents Fight Humanism," *Human Events*, 5 October 1986.

19. Paul Vitz, *Censorship: Evidence of Bias in Our Children's Textbooks* (Ann Arbor, MI: Servant Books, 1986), p. 1.

20. *Ibid*.

21. *Ibid.*

22. *Ibid.*

23. *Ibid*, p. 77.

24. Quoted by Charles L. Glenn, "Religion, Textbooks, and the Common School," *The Public Interest*, no. 88, (Summer 1987), p. 44.

25. Editorial, "Two Textbook Cases Assail Democracy," *Miami News*, 2 September 1987, p. 8a.

26. James Carper, "The Christian Day School Movement, 1960-1982," *The Educational Forum*, vol. 17, no. , (1983), p. 135.

27. Neal Devins, "State Regulation of Christian Schools," *Journal of Legislation*, vol. 10, (Summer 1983), p. 355.

28. *Ibid*, p. 356.

29. Carper, "The Christian Day School Movement," p. 281-282.

30. Alan N. Grover, *Ohio's Trojan Horse: A Warning to Christian Schools Everywhere* (Greenville, S.C.: Bob Jones University Press, Inc., 1977), p. xiv.

31. *Ibid*, p. 3.

32. *Ibid.*

33. *Wisconsin v. Yoder*, 406 U.S. 205 (1972), *Everson v. Board of Education*, 330 U.S. 1 (1947), *Pierce v. Society of Sisters*, 268 U.S. 510 (1925).

34. Quoted by Barbara R. Diehl, "The Right to Regulate Nonpublic Education," *Urban Lawyer*, vol. 15, (Winter 1983), p. 99.

35. *Ibid.*

36. James E. Carper and Neal E. Devins, "The State and the Christian Day School," *Religion and the State: Essays in Honor of Leo Pfeffer*, ed. James E. Wood, Jr. (Waco, Texas: Baylor University Press, 1985), pp. 217-218. Further discussion of state regulation of Christian schools can be found in: Neal Devins, "State Regulation of Christian Schools," *Journal of Legislation*, vol. 10, (Summer 1983), pp. 351-381; and Denise M. Bainton, "State Regulation of Private Religious Schools and the State's Interest in Education," *Arizona Law Review*, vol. 25, (1983), pp. 123-149.

37. *Ibid*, pp. 218-219.

37. *Ibid.*

39. *Kentucky State Board v. Rudasill*, 589 S.W. 2d 877 (1979). Of related interest see: *Hinton vs. Ky. St. Bd. of Educ.*, No. 88314 (Franklin Cir. Ct. Div. I,

Oct. 4, 1978). A detailed commentary on this second case is provided by Michael D. Baker, "Regulation of Fundamentalist Christian Schools: Free Exercise of Religion v. The State's Interest in Quality Education," *Kentucky Law Journal*, vol. 67, (1978-1979).

40. *State v. Whisner*, 351, N.E. 2d 750 (1976).

41. Quoted by Carper and Devins, "The State and the Christian Day School," p. 220.

42. *Douglas v. Faith Baptist Church*, 301 N.W. 2d 571 (Neb. 1981).

43. *State v. Shaver*, 294 N.W. 2d 883 (North Dakota, 1980).

44. Carper and Devins, "The State and the Christian Day School," p. 223.

45. *Ibid*, p. 224.

# CHAPTER 7

1. James E. Wood, Jr., "The Christianization of the Public Schools," p. 1. Paper presented at the National Meeting of the Anti-Defamation League of B'nai B'rith at New York City, May 31, 1984.

2. *Ibid*, p. 12. An extensive literature has developed since the 1950s describing the different dimensions of status politics. See Daniel Bell, "The New American Right," in Daniel Bell, ed. *The New American Right* (New York: Citation Books, 1955); Richard Hofstadter, "The Pseudo-Conservative Revolt," in Daniel Bell, ed., *The New American Right*; Seymour M. Lipset, "The Sources of the Radical Right," in Bell, ed., *The New American Right*. Lipset, *Political Man* (New York: 1960); Joseph R. Gusfield, *Symbolic Crusade* (Urbana, Ill.: University of Illinois Press, 1976); Louis R. Zurcher, *Citizens for Decency* (Austin: University of Texas Press, 1976) and Murray Edelman, *The Symbolic Uses of Politics* (Urbana, IL: University of Illinois Press, 1964); and Edelman, *Politics as Symbolic Action: Mass Arousal and Quiescence* (Chicago: Markham, 1971).

3. *Pride and Woodward*, p. 13.

4. Grant Wacker, "Searching for Norman Rockwell," p. 332 reprinted in Richard John Neuhaus and Michael Cromartie, *Piety & Politics: Evangelicals and Fundamentalists Confront the World* (New York: Ethics and Public Policy Center, 1987).

5. *Ibid*, p. 333.

6. Alan Peshkin, *God's Choice: The Total World of a Fundamentalist Christian School* (Chicago: University of Chicago Press, 1986), p. 257.

7. *Ibid*.

8. *Ibid.*

9. *Ibid*, p. 258.

10. *Ibid*, p. 259.

11. Quoted by Wood, "The Christianization," p. 2.

12. *Ibid.*

13. Lawrence A. Cremin, *American Education: The Colonial Experience, 1607-1783* (New York: Harper Torchbooks, 1970), p. 442.

14. Quoted by Wood, "The Christianization," p. 4.

15. Peshkin, *God's Choice*, p. 298.

16. *Ibid.*

17. *Ibid.*

18. Deborah Byrnes and Gary Kiger, "Religious Prejudice and Democracy: Conflict in the Classroom," *Issues in Education*, vol. 4, no. 2, (Fall, 1986), p. 167.

19. Flo Conway and Jim Siegelman, *Holy Terror: The Fundamentalist War on America's Freedoms in Religion, Politics and Our Private Lives* (Garden City, N.Y.: Doubleday & Company, 1982), p. 116.

20. Quoted by Nelkin, *op. cit.*, p. 149.

21. Henry M. Morris, *Education for the Real World* (San Diego: Creation Life Publishers, 1978), p. 28.

22. Onalee McGraw, *Family Choice in Education: The New Imperative* (Washington, D.C.: The Heritage Foundation, 1978), p. 10.

23. Rousas J. Rushdoony in the Introduction to Alan N. Grover's *Ohio's Trojan Horse* (Greenville, S.C.: Bob Jones University Press, Inc., 1977), p. xiv.

24. Robert Allen Hill and Olaf John, *Your Children: The Victims of Public Education* (Van Nuys, Calif.: Bible Voice, Inc., 1978), pp. 27-28.

25. Morris, *Education for the Real World*, p. 9.

26. Byrnes and Kiger, "Religious Prejudice," p. 168.

# Bibliography

Alexander, Kern. *School Law*. St. Paul, MN: West Publishing Company, 1980.

Arons, Stephen. *Compelling Belief: The Culture of American Schooling*. New York: McGraw-Hill Book Company, 1983.

Association for Supervision and Curriculum Development. *Religion in the Curriculum*. Washington: Association for Supervision and Curriculum Development, 1987.

Bainton, Denise M. "State Regulation of Private Religious Schools and the State's Interest in Education." *Arizona Law Review* 25 (1983): 123-149.

Baker, Michael D. "Regulation of Fundamentalist Christian Schools: Free Exercise of Religion v. The State's Interest in Quality Education." *Kentucky Law Journal* 67 (1978-1979): 415-429.

Ball, William R. "Opting Out of Reading Class in Tennessee: The Only Possible Outcome." *Education Week*, 3 December 1986.

Barr, James. *Fundamentalism*. Philadelphia, Pa.: The Westminster Press, 1978.

Binder, Thomas. "Douglas v. Faith Baptist Church Under Constitutional Scrutiny." *Nebraska Law Review* 61 (Spring 1982): 74-97.

Bird, Wendell. "Freedom of Religion and Science Instruction in Public Schools." *Yale Law Journal* 83 (1978).

Bollier, David. *Liberty and Justice for Some: Defending a Free Society from the Radical Right's Holy War on Democracy*. Washington, D.C.: People for the American Way, 1982.

———. *The Witch Hunt Against "Secular Humanism"*. Washington: People for the American Way, 1983.

Burress, Lee and Edward Jenkinson. *The Student's Right to Know*. Urbana, Illinois, National Council of English Teachers, 1982.

Butts, R. Freeman. *Religion, Education and the First Amendment: The Appeal to History.* Washington, D.C.: People for the American Way, 1986.

Byrnes, Deborah and Gary Kiger. "Religious Prejudice and Democracy: Conflict in the Classroom," *Issues in Education* 4, no. 2 (Fall 1986): 167-176.

California State Advisory Committee on Science Education. *Science Framework for California Public Schools. Kindergarten—Grades One through Twelve.* Sacramento, Calif.: California State Department of Education, 1969.

Campbell, Colin. "Book Banning in America." *New York Times Book Review,* 20 December 1981).

Cannon, Lou. "Hill Gets Reagan's Prayer Amendment," *The Washington Post,* 18 May 1982.

Carper, James. "The Christian Day School Movement 1960-1982," *The Educational Forum* 47 (Winter 1983): 135-149.

Carper, James E. and Neal E. Devins, "The State and the Christian Day School." In *Religion and the State: Essays in Honor of Leo Pfeffer,* edited by James E. Wood Jr., Waco, Tex.: Baylor University Press, 1985.

Ciolli, Rita. "The Politics of Textbooks," *APF Reporter* 7, no. 1 (Winter 1984).

Cole, Stewart G. *The History of Fundamentalism.* Hamden, Conn.: Archon Books, 1963.

Conway, Flo and Jim Siegelman. *Holy Terror: The Fundamentalist War on America's Freedoms in Religion, Politics and Our Private Lives.* Garden City, N.Y.: Doubleday and Company, 1982.

Coons, John E. and Stephen D. Sugarman. *Education by Choice: The Case for Family Control.* Berkeley, Calif.: University of California Press, 1978.

Crawford, Alan. *Thunder on the Right: "The New Right and the Politics of Resentment.* New York: Pantheon, 1981.

Cremin, Lawrence A. *American Education: The Colonial Experience, 1607-1783.* New York: Harper Torchbooks, 1970.

Devins, Neal. "State Regulation of Christian Schools," *Journal of Legislation* 10 (Summer, 1983): 351-381.

Dewey, John. *Democracy and Education: An Introduction to the Philosophy of Education.* New York: The Free Press, 1966.

Diehl, Barbara R. "The Right to Regulate Nonpublic Education." *Urban Lawyer* 15 (Winter, 1983): 97-111.

Duncan, Homer. *Secular Humanism.* Lubbock: Missionary Crusader, 1980.

Egerton, John. "The Battle for the Books." *The Progressive* 39, no. 6 (June 1975): 13-17.

Elson, Ruth Miller. *Guardians of Tradition: American Schoolbooks in the Nineteenth Century.* Lincoln: University of Nebraska Press, 1964.

Falwell, Jerry. *America Can Be Saved.* Murfreesboro, Tenn.: Sword of the Lord Publishers, 1979.

Falwell, Jerry, Ed Dobson and Ed Hindson, editors. *The Fundamentalist Phenomenon: The Resurgence of Conservative Christianity.* Garden City, N.Y.: Doubleday-Galilee Original, 1981.

Fitzgerald, Frances. *America Revised: History Schoolbooks in the Twentieth Century.* New York: Vintage Books, 1980.

Flygare, Thomas J. "The Case of Segraves v. State of California." *Phi Delta Kappan* 63, no. 2 (October 1981): 98-99.

Franklin Circuit Court, Division I. *Hinton v. Kentucky State Board of Education,* 88314 (October 4, 1978).

Frishman, Bob. *American Families: Responding to the Pro-Family Movement.* Washington: People for the American Way, 1984.

Gabler, Mel and Norma. "Where is the Public in Public Education." *Phi Delta Kappan* 64 (October 1982): 96-97.

———. *Humanism in Textbooks: Secular Religion in the Classroom.* Longview, Tex.: The Mel Gablers, P.O. Box 7518, 1983.

Gardner, Eileen, editor. *A New Agenda for Education.* Washington: The Heritage Foundation, 1985.

———. "A Parent's Guide to Textbook Review and Reform." Special Supplement to *Education Update* (Winter 1978) Washington, D.C.: The Heritage Foundation.

Gell-Mann, Murray, "First Word," *Omni* 9, no. 5 (February 1987): 8.

Gish, Duane. "Creation-Evolution," in Henry M. Morris, Duane T. Gish and George M. Hillestad *Creation: Acts, Facts and Impacts.* San Diego: Creation Life Publishers, 1974.

———. *Evolution? The Fossils Say No!* San Diego: Creation Life Publishers, 1972.

Glenn, Charles L. "Religion, Textbooks, and the Common School." *The Public Interest* 88 (Summer 1987): 28-47.

Gould, Stephen Jay. *Ever Since Darwin.* New York: Norton Press, 1977.

Grover, Alan N. *Ohio's Trojan Horse: A Warning to Christian Schools Every-where.* Greenville, S.C.: Bob Jones University Press, Inc., 1977.

Hefley, James C. *Are Textbooks Harming Your Children? Norma and Mel Gabler Take Action and Show You How!* Milford, MI: Mott Media, 1979.

Herr, Ethel. *Schools: How Parents Can Make a Difference.* Chicago: Moody Press, 1981.

Hill, Robert Allen and Olaf John. *Your Children: The Victims of Public Education.* Van Nuys, CA: Bible Voice, Inc., 1978.

Hill, Samuel S. and Dennis E. Owen. *The New Religious Political Right in America.* Nashville: Abington, 1982.

Hofstader, Richard. *Anti-Intellectualism in American Life.* New York: 1962.

Hook, Sidney, B.F. Skinner and Isaac Asimov. *Humanist Manifestos I and II.* New York, N.Y.: Prometheus Books, 1973.

Jenkinson, Edward B. *The Schoolbook Protest Movement: 40 Questions & Answers.* Bloomington, IN: Phi Delta Kappa, 1986.

————. *Censors in the Classroom: The Mind Benders.* Carbondale, IL: Southern Illinois University Press, 1979.

————. *The Tale of Tell City: An Anti-Censorship Saga.* Washington: People for the American Way, 1983.

Kentucky Supreme Court. *Kentucky State Board v. Rudasill,* 589 S.W. 2d 877 (1979).

LaHaye, Tim. *The Battle for the Public Schools.* Old Tappan, N.J.: Fleming H. Revell Company, 1983.

————. *The Battle for the Mind.* Old Tappan, New Jersey: Fleming H. Revell Company, 1980.

Larson, Edward J. *Trial and Error: The American Controversy Over Creation and Evolution.* New York, N.Y.: Oxford University Press, 1985.

Lester, Julius. "Morality and Education." *Democracy,* (April 1982).

The MacNeil-Lehrer Report, "The Texas Textbook Debate." 10 November 1982.

Maquire, Daniel C. *The New Subversives: Anti-Americanism of the Religious Right.* New York: The Continuum Publishing Co., 1982.

Marsden, George M. *Fundamentalism and American Culture, the Shaping of Twentieth-Century Evangelicalism: 1870-1925.* New York: Oxford University Press, 1980.

Marshner, Connaught. *Blackboard Tyranny.* New Rochelle, N.Y.: Arlington House, 1978.

Martin, William. "The Guardians Who Slumbereth Not." *Texas Monthly* (November 1982): 145-150.

McGraw, Onalee. *Secular Humanism and the Schools: The Issues Whose Time Has Come.* Washington, D.C.: The Heritage Foundation, 1976.

——. *Family Choice in Education: The New Imperative.* Washington, D.C.: The Heritage Foundation, 1978.

——. "Who is Censoring Books? The Debate Continues." *Education Update* 6, no. 4 (October 1982).

——. "Where is the Public in Public Education." *Phi Delta Kappan,* 64, (October 1982): 94-96.

McIntyre, Thomas J. *The Fear Brokers.* New York: The Pilgrim Press, 1979.

McLoughlin. "Is there a Third Force in Christendom?" *Dadelus* 96 (Winter 1967): 43-68.

Editorial. "Two Textbook Cases Assail Democracy." *Miami News,* 2 September 1987): 8a.

Moore, John A. "Creation in California." *Dadelus* (Summer 1974): 173-189.

*Morris, Barbara M. "The Real Issue in Education as Seen by a Journalist on the Far Right." Phi Delta Kappan 61, no. 9, 613-615.*

——. *Change Agents in the Schools.* Upland, Calif.: The Barbara M. Morris Report, 1979.

——. *The National Educator,* July, 1977.

——. *Scientific Creationism.* San Diego, Calif.: Creation Life Publishers, 1972.

——. *Introducing Scientific Creationism into the Public Schools.* San Diego, CA: Institute for Creation Research, 1975.

Morris, Henry M. *Education for the Real World.* San Diego, Calif.: Creation Life Publishers, 1977.

——. "Evolution, Creation and the Public Schools." In *Creation: Acts, Facts and Impacts,* edited by Henry M. Morris, Duane T. Gish and George M. Hillestad. San Diego, CA: Creation Life Publishers, 1974.

Moyer, Waynes A. *Scopes Revisited: Evolution v. Biblical Creationism.* Washington, D.C.: People for the American Way, 1983.

Nebraska Supreme Court. *State v. Faith Baptist Church,* 301 N.W. 2d 571 9 (1981).

Neuhaus, Richard John and Michael Cromartie, eds. *Piety & Politics: Evangelicals and Fundamentalists Confront the World.* New York: Ethics and Public Policy Center, 1987.

Nelkin, Dorothy. *The Creation Controversy: Science or Scripture in the Schools.* New York: W.W. Norton & Company, 1982.

Nietz, John. *Old Textbooks.* Pittsburgh, Pa.: University of Pittsburgh Press, 1961.

Nocera, Joseph. "The Big Book Banning Brawl," *The New Republic,* 13 September 1982): 20-25.

North Dakota Supreme Court. *State v. Shaver,* 294 N.W. 2d 883 (1980).

O'Neil, Robert. *Classrooms in the Crossfire: The Rights and Interests of Students, Parents, Teachers, Administrators, Librarians and the Community.* Bloomington, IN: Indiana University Press, 1981.

Ohio Supreme Court. *State v. Whisner,* 351, N.E. 2d 750 (1976).

Park, Charles J. "Preachers, Politics, and Public Education: A Review of Right-Wing Pressures Against Public Schooling in America." *Phi Delta Kappan* 61 (May 1980): 608-612.

Parker, Barbara. "Your Schools May be in the Next Battlefield in the Crusade Against 'Improper' Textbooks." *The American School Board Journal* 166 (June 1979): 21-26.

Parker, Barbara and Stefanie Weiss. *Protecting the Freedom to Learn: A Citizen's Guide.* Washington, D.C.: People for the American Way, 1986.

Parker, Franklin. *The Battle of the Books: Kanawha County.* Bloomington, IN: Phi Delta Kappa, 1975.

People for the American Way. *Attacks on Freedom to Learn: A 1984-1985 Report.* Washington, D.C.: People for the American Way, 1986.

Peshkin, Alan. *God's Choice: The Total World of a Fundamentalist Christian School.* Chicago: University of Chicago Press, 1986.

Rafferty, Max. Superintendent of Public Instruction. *Guidelines for Moral Instruction in California: A Report Accepted by the State Board of Education* May 9, 1969. Sacramento, CA: California State Department of Education.

Raths, Louise E., Merrill Harmin and Sidney B. Simon. *Values and Teaching.* Columbus: Charles E. Merrill Publishing Co., 1966.

Ravitch, Diane. "The New Right and the Schools." *American Educator* 6, no. 3 (Fall 1982): 8-13, 46.

—— . "Confronting New Right Attacks on Public Education," *Education Digest* 48 (March 1983): 6-9.

Raywid, Maryann. *The Ax-Grinders, Critics of Our Public Schools.* New York: Macmillan and Co., 1962.

Rushdoony, Rousas J. *Intellectual Schizophrenia: Culture, Crisis and Education.* Philadelphia: The Presbytarian and Reformed Publishing Company, 1973. 1973.

—— . *The Messianic Character of American Education: Studies in the History of the Philosophy of Education.* Nutley, N.J.: The Craig Press, 1972.

Russell, Charles Allyn. *Voices of American Fundamentalism: Seven Biographical Studies.* Philadelphia: The Westminster Press, 1976.

Saltsman, Robert. "State v. Whisner: State Minimum Educational Standards and Non-Public Religious Schools." *Ohio Northern University Law Review* 4 (July 1977): 710-719.

Sandeen, Ernest R. *The Roots of Fundamentalism: British and American Millenerianism, 1800-1930.* Chicago, Ill.: The University of Chicago Press, 1970.

Schaeffer, Francis A. *How Should We Then Live: The Rise and Decline of Western Culture and Thought.* Old Tappan, N.J.: Fleming H. Revell Company, 1976.

—— . *A Christian Manifesto.* Westchester, IL: Crossway Books, 1981.

Schafly, Phyllis. "Alabama Parents Fight Humanism." *Human Events* (5 October 1986).

—— . "Fact and Fiction About Censorship," Washington, D.C.: National Defense Committee, National Society, Daughters of the American Revolution, 1984.

Siegel, Harvey. "Creationism, Evolution, and Education: The California Fiasco." *Phi Delta Kappan* 63, no. 2 (October 1981): 95-101.

Simon, Sidney B., Leland W. Howe, and Howard Kirschenbaum. *Values Clarification: A Handbook of Practical Strategies for Teachers and Students.* New York: Hart Publishing Company, 1972.

US District Court Eastern District of Arkansas Western Division, William R. Overton, US District Judge, *McLean v. the Arkansas Board of Education et al.,* (January 5, 1982).

US Supreme Court. *Edwards, Governors of Louisiana, et al. v. Aquillard et al.,* N. 85-1513. Argued December 10, 1986-Decided June 19, 1987.

—— . *Wisconsin v. Yoder,* 406 U.S. 205 (1972).

————. *School District of Abington Township v. Schempp and Murray v. Curlett*, 374 U.S. 203, 83 SCt. 1560 (1963).

————. *Engle v. Vitale*, 370 U.S. 421, 82, S.Ct. 1261 (1962).

————. *Everson v. Board of Education*, 330 U.S. 1, 67 S.Ct. 504 (1947).

————. *Pierce v. Society of the Sisters of the Holy Names of Jesus and Mary*, 268 U.S. 510, 45 S.Ct. 571 (1925).

Vitz, Paul C. *Censorship: Evidence of Bias in Our Children's Textbooks*. Ann Arbor, MI: Servant Books, 1986.

Viviano, Frank. "The Crucifixion of Evolution: What Your Kids Will be Learning this Fall." *Mother Jones* (September/October, 1981).

Weissmann, Ann. "Building the Tower of Babel." *Texas Outlook* 65, no. 4 (Winter 1981-82): 10-15, 29.

Whitehead, John W. and John Conlan. "The Establishment of the Religion of Secular Humanism and Its First Amendment Implications." *Texas Tech Law Review* 10, no. 1 (1979).

Will, George F. "Opposing Prefab Prayer." *Newsweek*, 7 June 1982): 84.

Wood, James E. "The Christianization of the Public Schools." Paper presented at the national meeting of the Anti-Defamation League of B'nai B'rith, New York City, 31 May 1984.

Woodward, Kenneth and Eloise Saholz. "The Right's New Bogeyman." *Newsweek*, (6 July 1981): 48, 50.

# Index